WHAT I THOUGHT I SAW

new york • london

PHOTOGRAPHS BY KELLI BICKMAN

YATRA PUBLICATIONS / 11:11 STUDIO

Published by

Yatra Publications
218 Mill Street West
Cannon Falls, MN 55009
fax 1 (507) 263-0166

and

11:11 Studio
PO Box 208-kb
Old Chelsea Station
New York, NY 10113-0208

Printed in the United States of America
by IntraNet - Mpls, MN 55436

First Edition, 1996
ISBN 1-889644-03-X
Library of Congress Catalog Card Number - 96-090532

For my two families...

The Bickmans
and
The Gaimans

I love you all very much.

kb

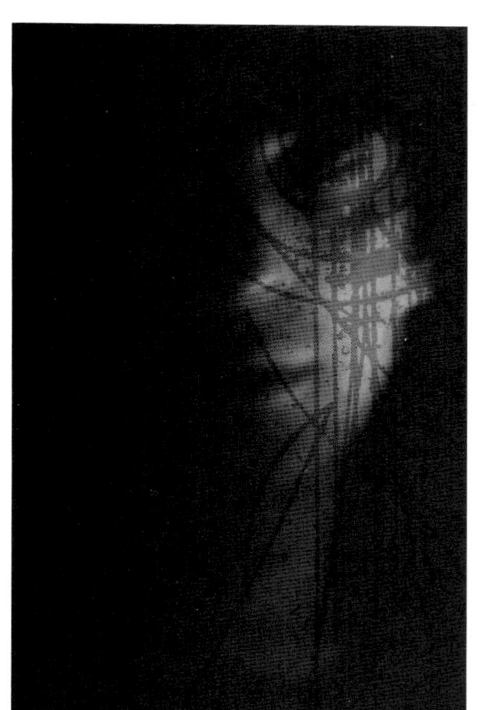
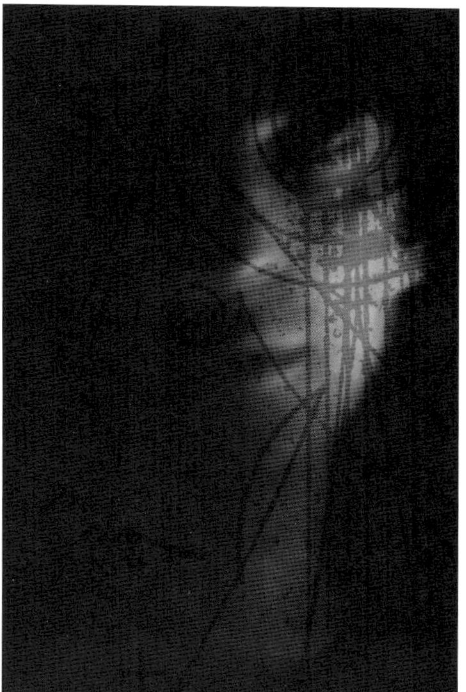
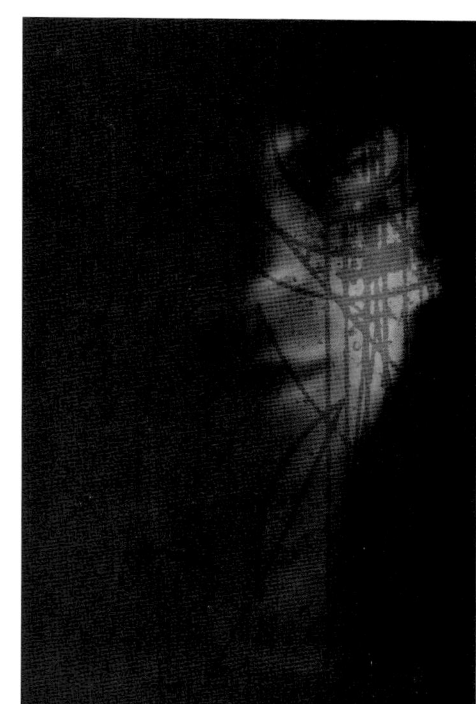

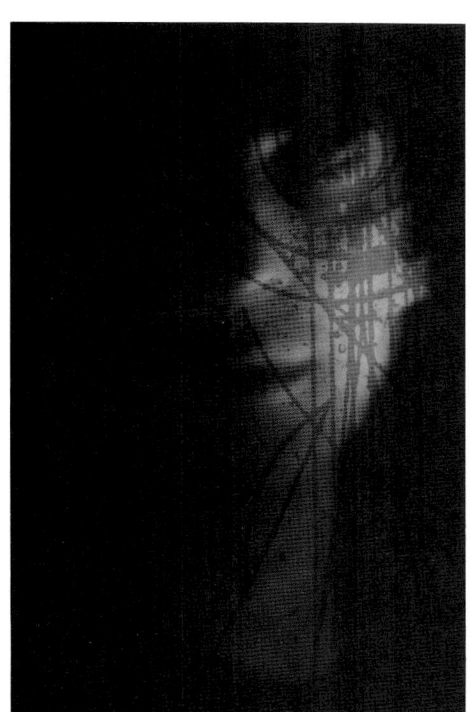
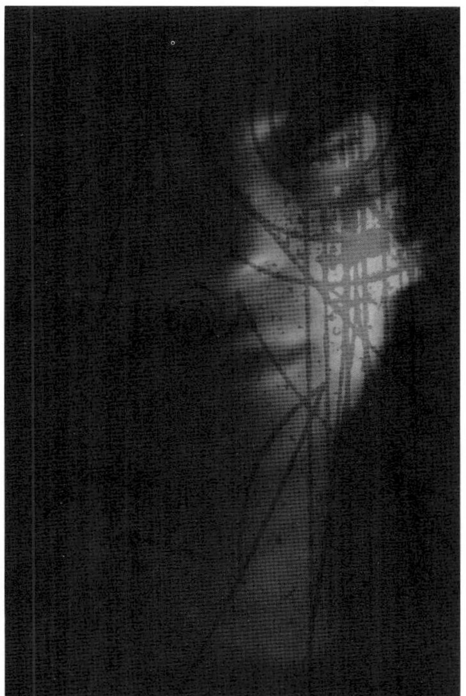
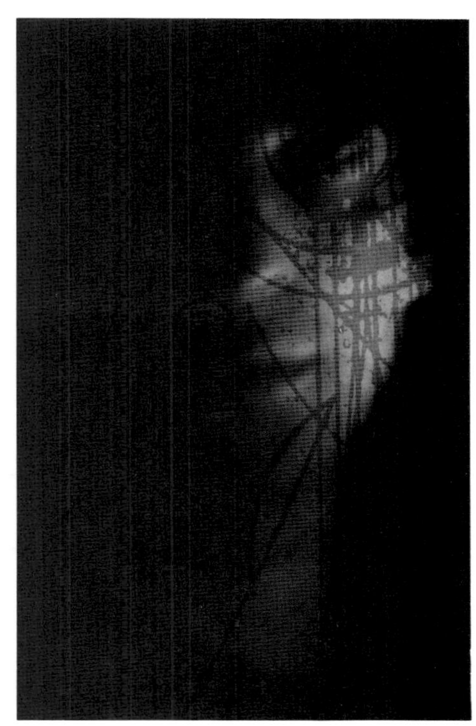

A GAME OF VIEW
Neil Gaiman, 1995

INTRODUCTION

True Stories: the Secret Life of Kelli Bickman

This is what Kelli Bickman looks like: she's skinny and witchy, with changeable hair (currently it's a punk and probably self-hacked Louise Brooks, dyed a shade of red never seen in nature) and her nose is slightly crooked (I know this because she told me; it is not noticeable, unless she tells you) and she has the most secretive smile of any human being alive. It's the smile of someone who knows all your secrets and is never going to breathe a word about any of them.

She may, on the other hand, take photographs.

She lives in New York, in the Village, in an apartment hung with strange cool art, dead-painted dolls and things that she found discarded and has rescued from the rubbish. I've only ever visited her apartment once. While I was there, the largest cockroach I have ever seen darted out from under a seat-cushion, and Kelli trapped it in a wine glass, and put it in a tupperware container, and sprayed fixative on it. I suppose it will wind up in an art-construction of some kind, on her wall.

I keep things for Kelli that I find in the woods: dead animals and old door keys and insects.

She is, however, neither grotesque nor gothic in her temperament: she is more or less unfailingly good-tempered. And she is an artist.

Sometimes I take all the credit for Kelli being a photographer. I say, "A couple of years ago, I decided that I needed to learn a new skill, so I bought myself a camera, and resolved to take a number of photographs in the woods behind my house; and I asked Kelli if she would help me. She had not used a camera for some years. We spent a few weeks taking photographs in the snow, by the end of which two things were apparent; firstly that I was no photographer, and, secondly, that Kelli was."

She rejects this as simplistic and wrong, pointing out that I wasn't that bad a photographer, and that she had studied photography in London some years earlier; and really, if I had any function at all in all that, it was simply to reinfect her with the joy of the darkroom and the black-and-white image.

And, reinfected, she went to New York. In her day job she works as Chris Claremont's assistant. The rest of the time, she is an artist and photographer. Perhaps she inherits some of her eye for a picture from her mother, Connie, a photographer and author; perhaps she is entirely self-created: a Frankenstein's monster with a crooked nose and a witchy twinkle.

This is how you can tell a real photographer: mostly, a real photographer does not say "I wish I had my camera on me right now". Instead a real photographer pulls out her camera and takes the photograph. Several of the photographs in this book are photos of this nature.

Early in 1996 I went to London for the filming of Neverwhere, my television series, and, after a month, I borrowed Kelli from Chris Claremont for two weeks, during which time she organized all the paper in the house, typed out the first two chapters of Neverwhere: The Novel, from my handwriting (which is not unreadable. I prefer to think of it as legibly challenged), and took many photographs of the cast and the crew and the many wonderful extras.

A number of the photographs in this book were taken at that time, and the idea for this book was also hatched then.

People who know me find it hard to equate the generally pleasant, good-natured, and more or less amiable fellow they meet with the driven crackpot who writes the fiction. I, for my part, have no idea how someone so sweet, and so perpetually amused, could take photographs that range from the gentle and tender through to the scabrous and the nightmarish, from high art to low documentary, and vice versa.

She has a secretive smile, though. I am sure that that accounts for an awful lot.

She says that this is what she thought she saw.

Personally, I don't believe a word of it.

Neil Gaiman
Somewhere in America
July 24, 1996

NEIL AND MADDY
1995

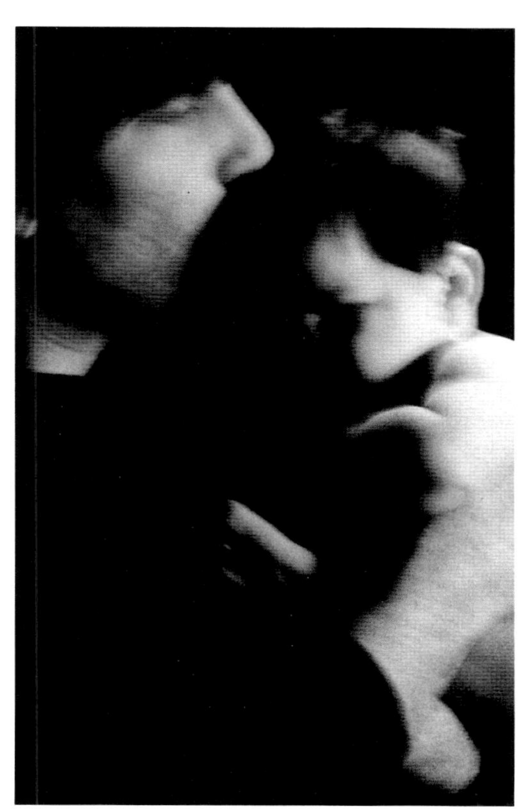

MISS UNDERSTOOD
New York

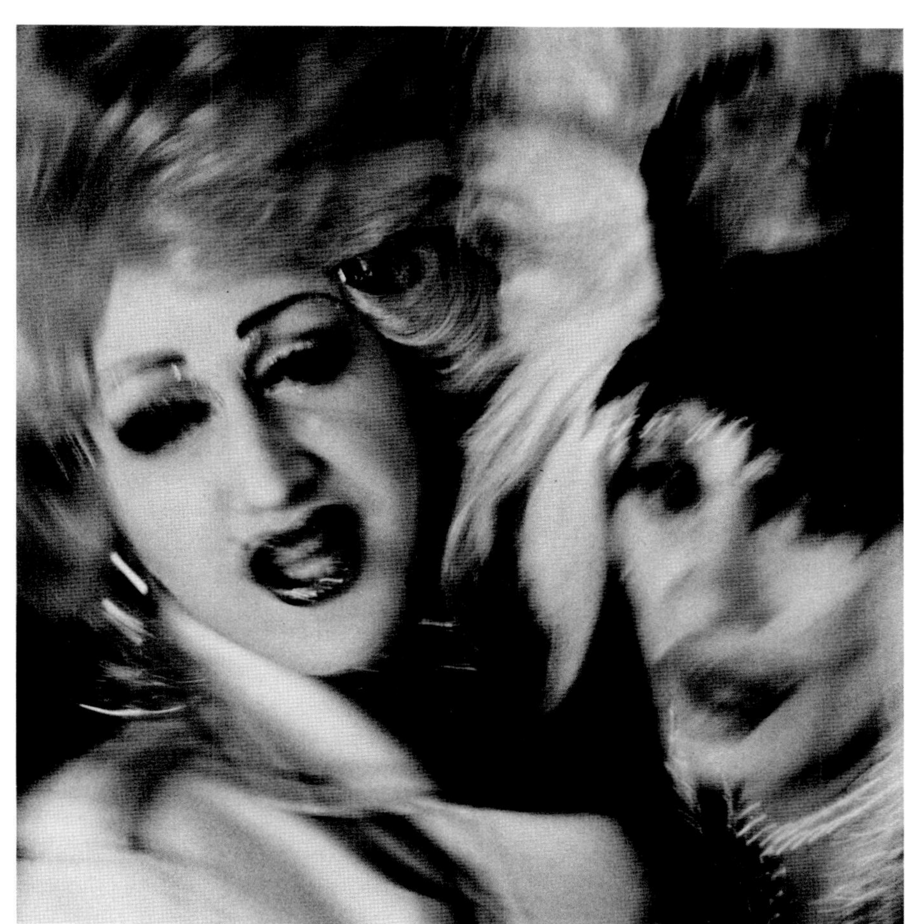

HEDY LAVERNE
New York

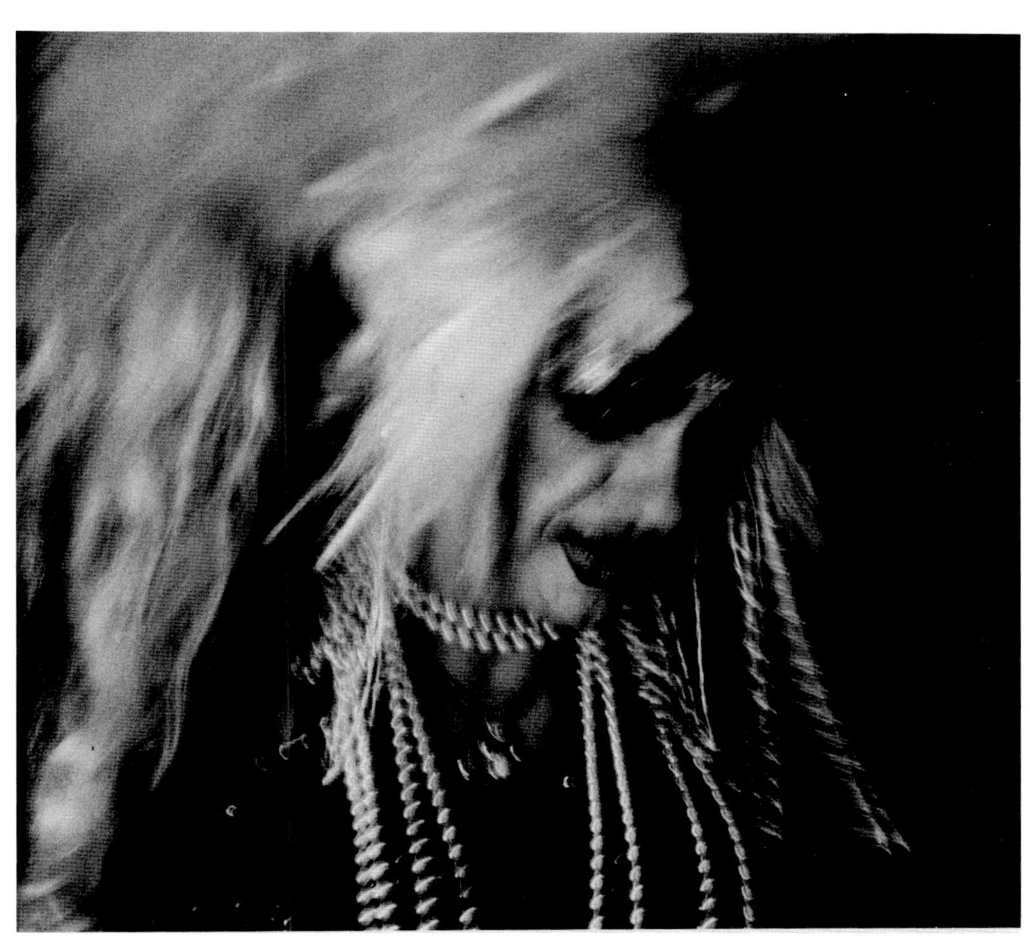

LUCRECIA
London

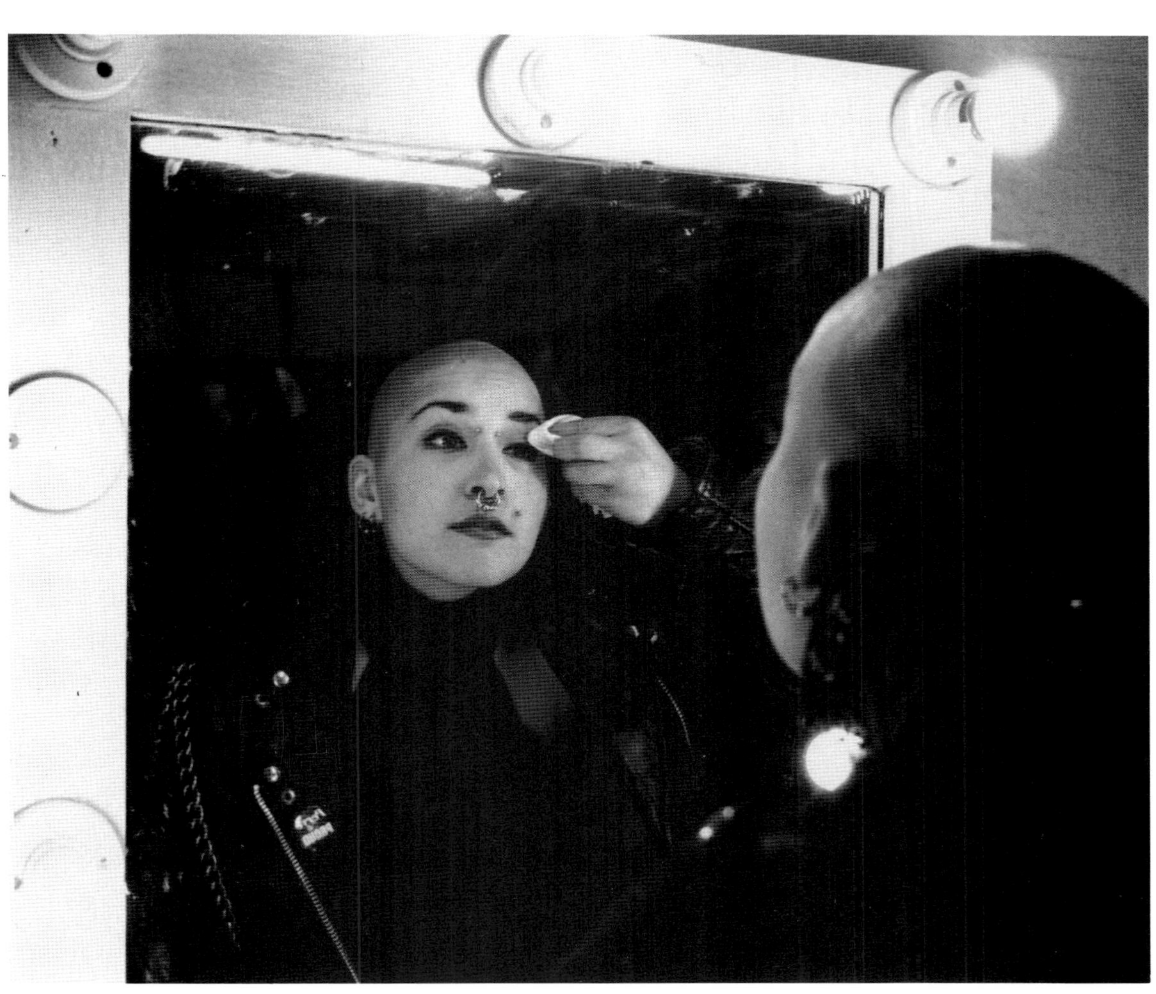

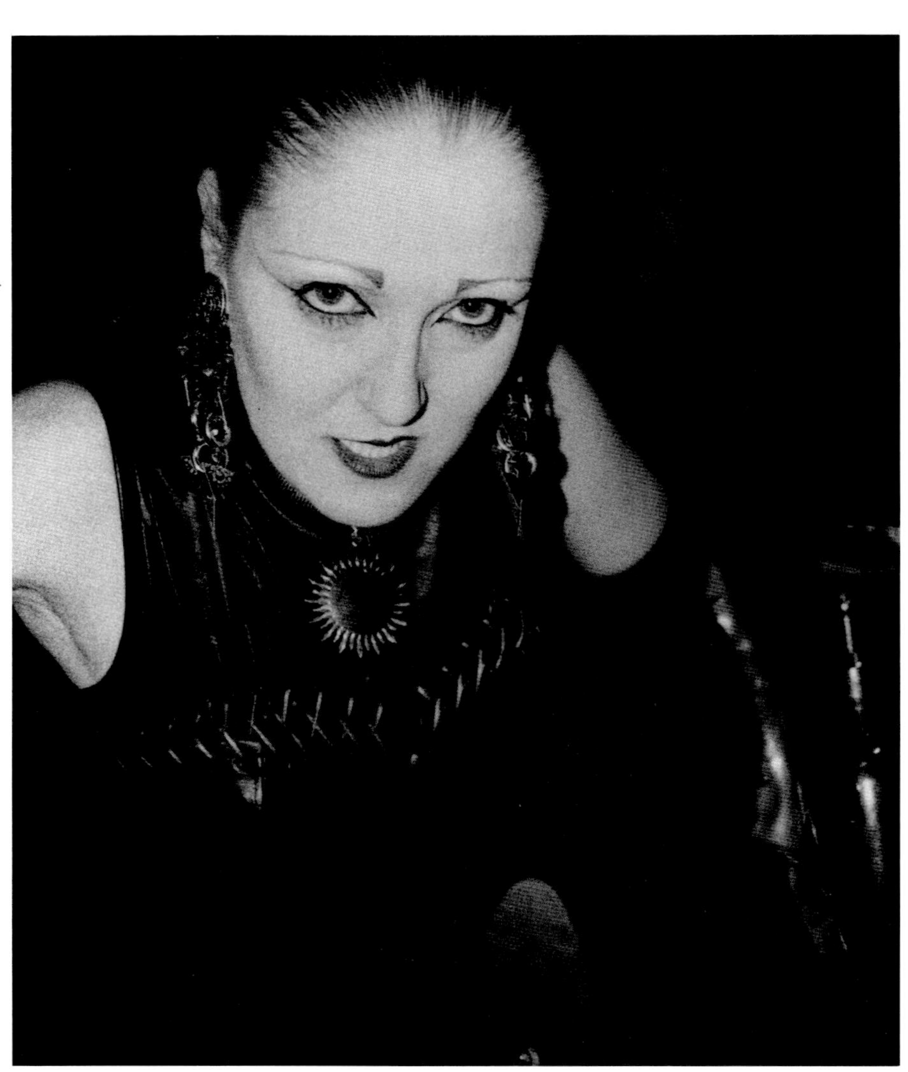

DONNA IN LEATHER
London

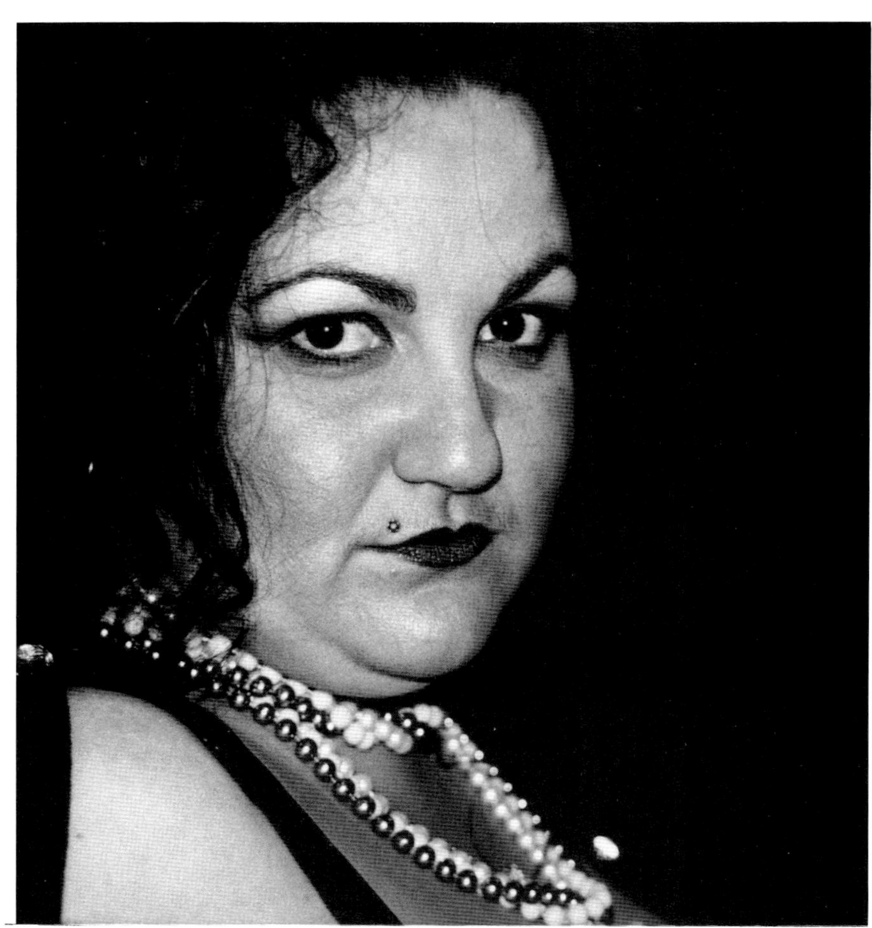

PEARLS
London

LUNCH
London

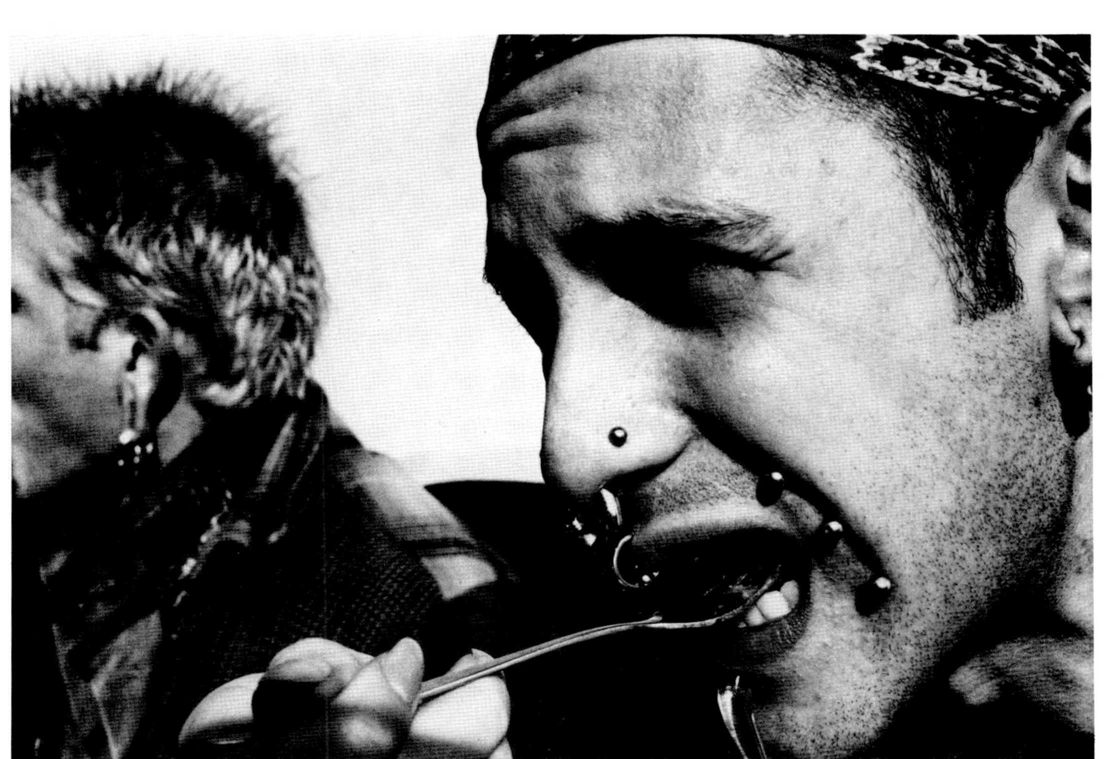

EVOLUTION
London

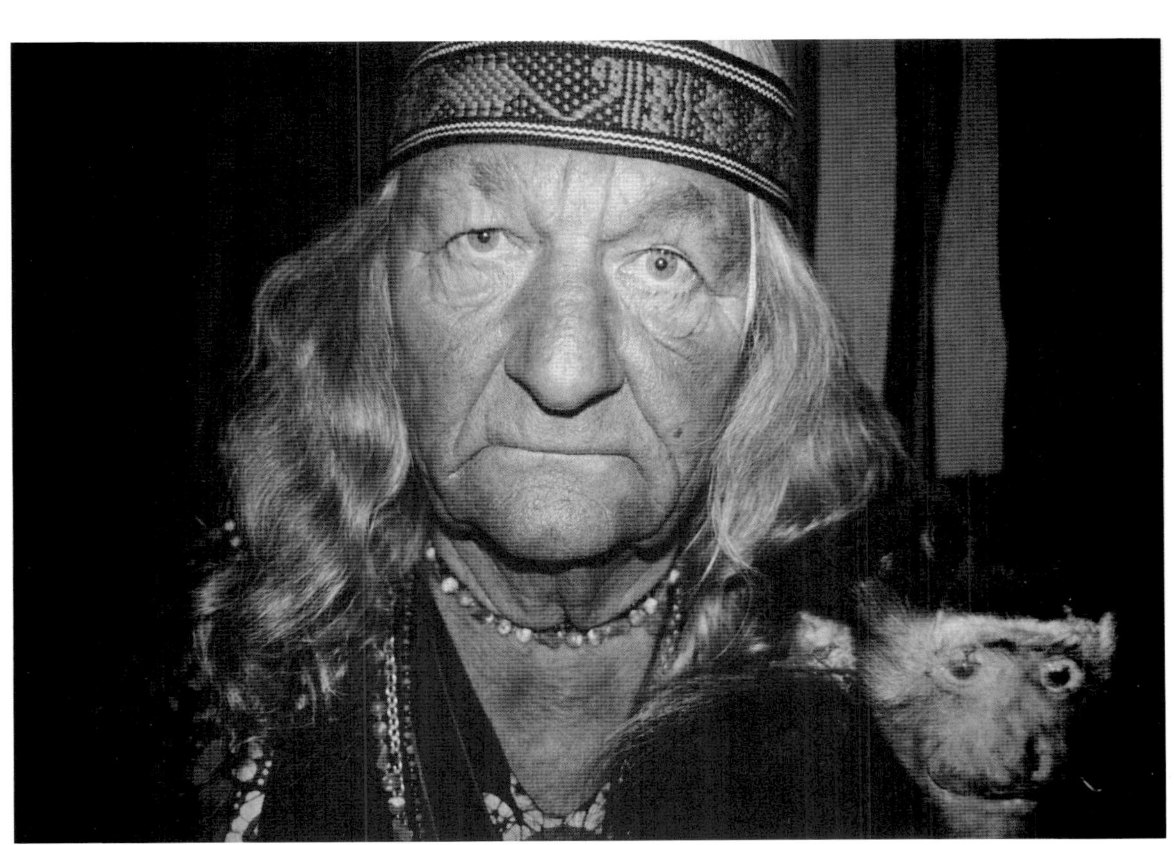

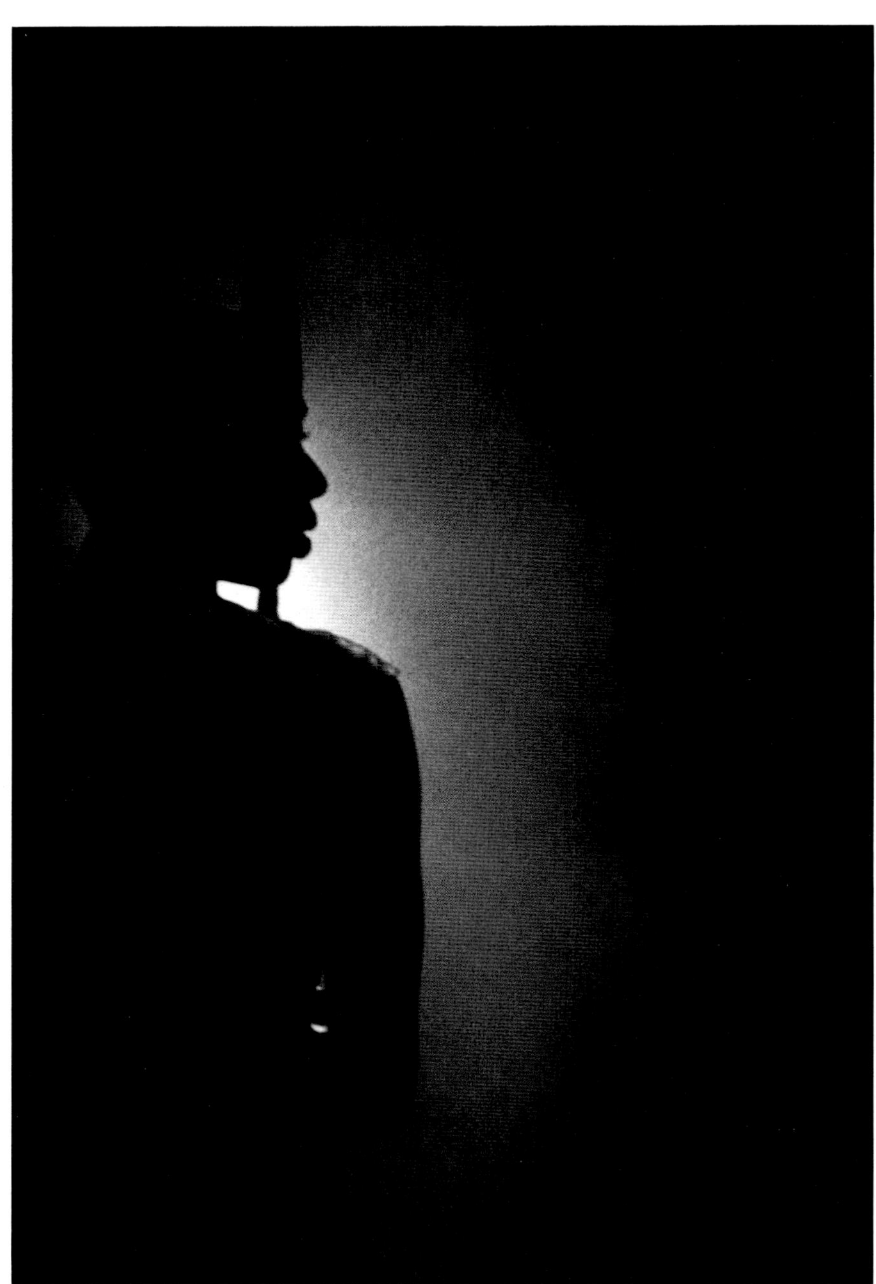

HUNTER
London

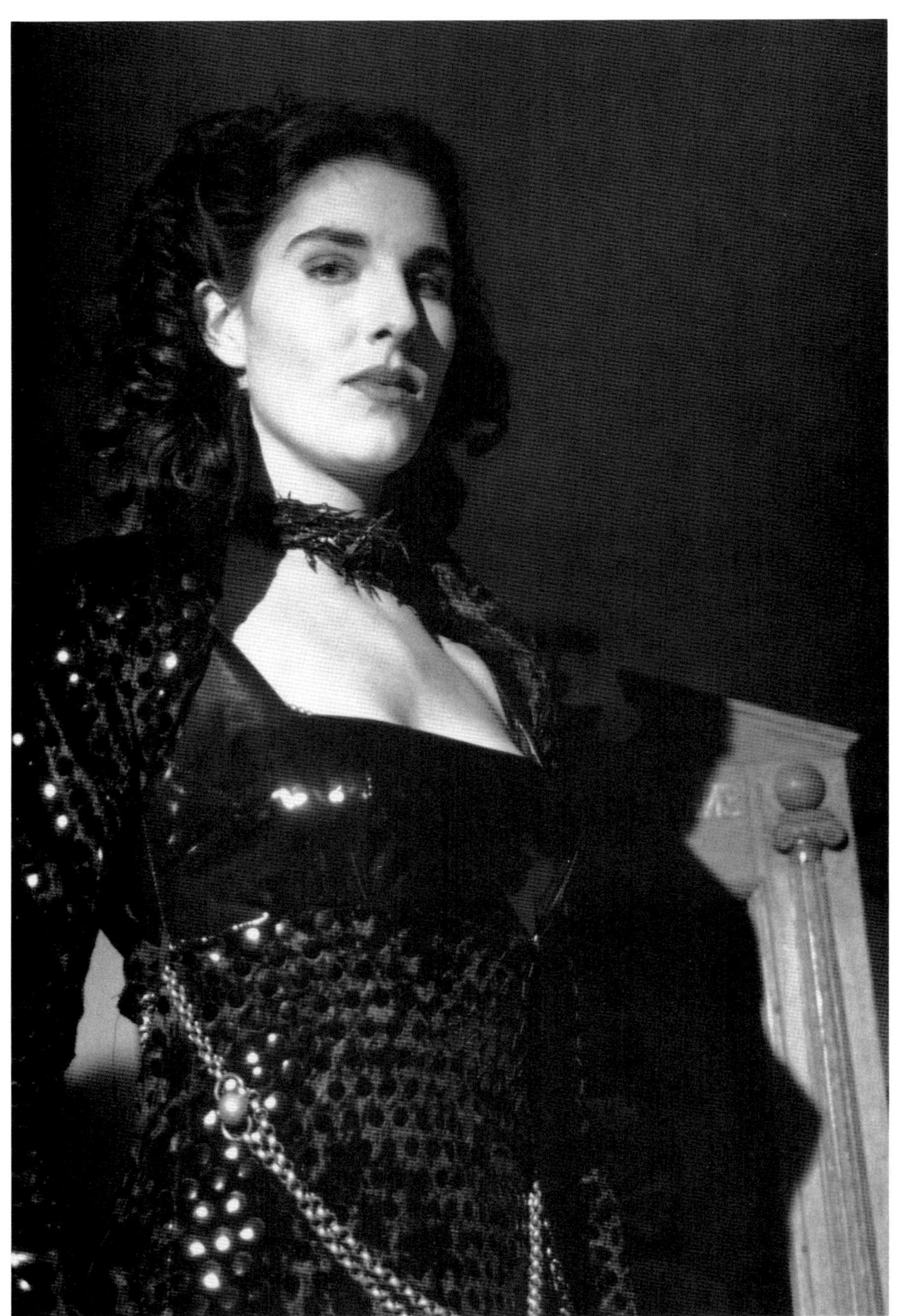

LAMIA
London

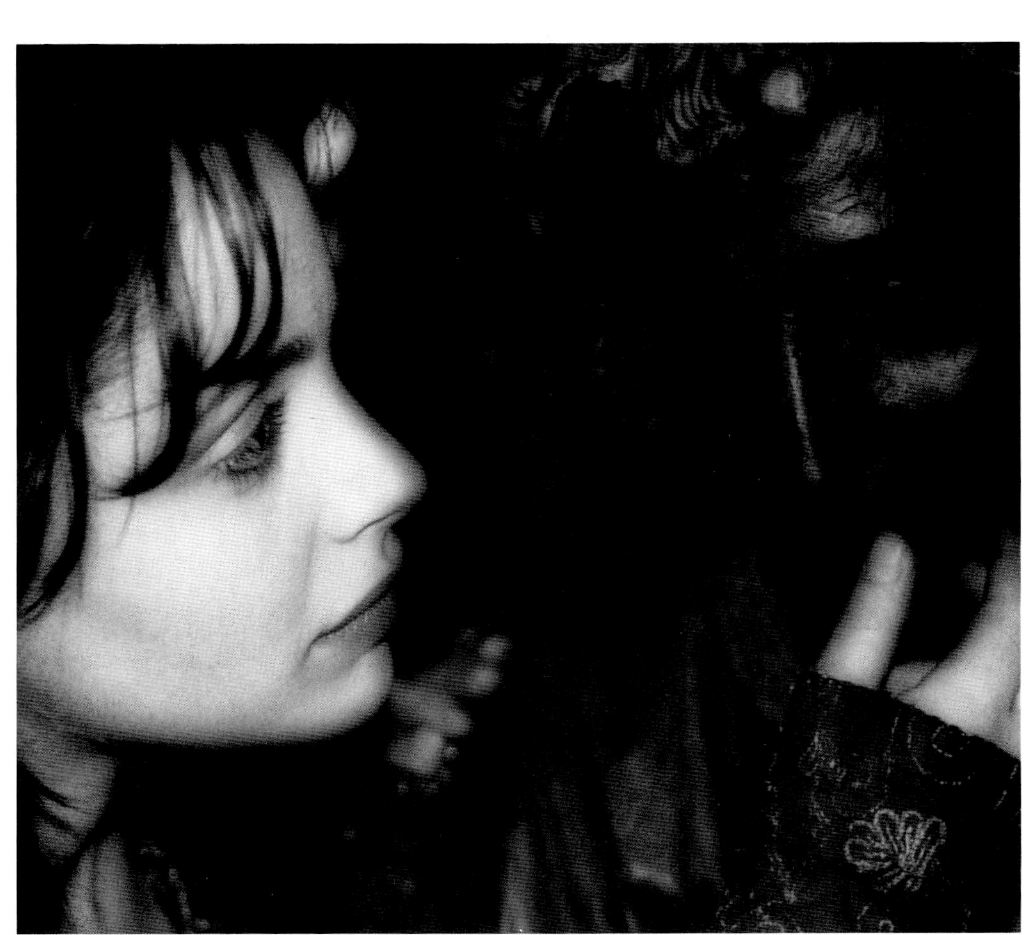

VISIT FROM AN ANGEL
London

RICHARD / GARY
London

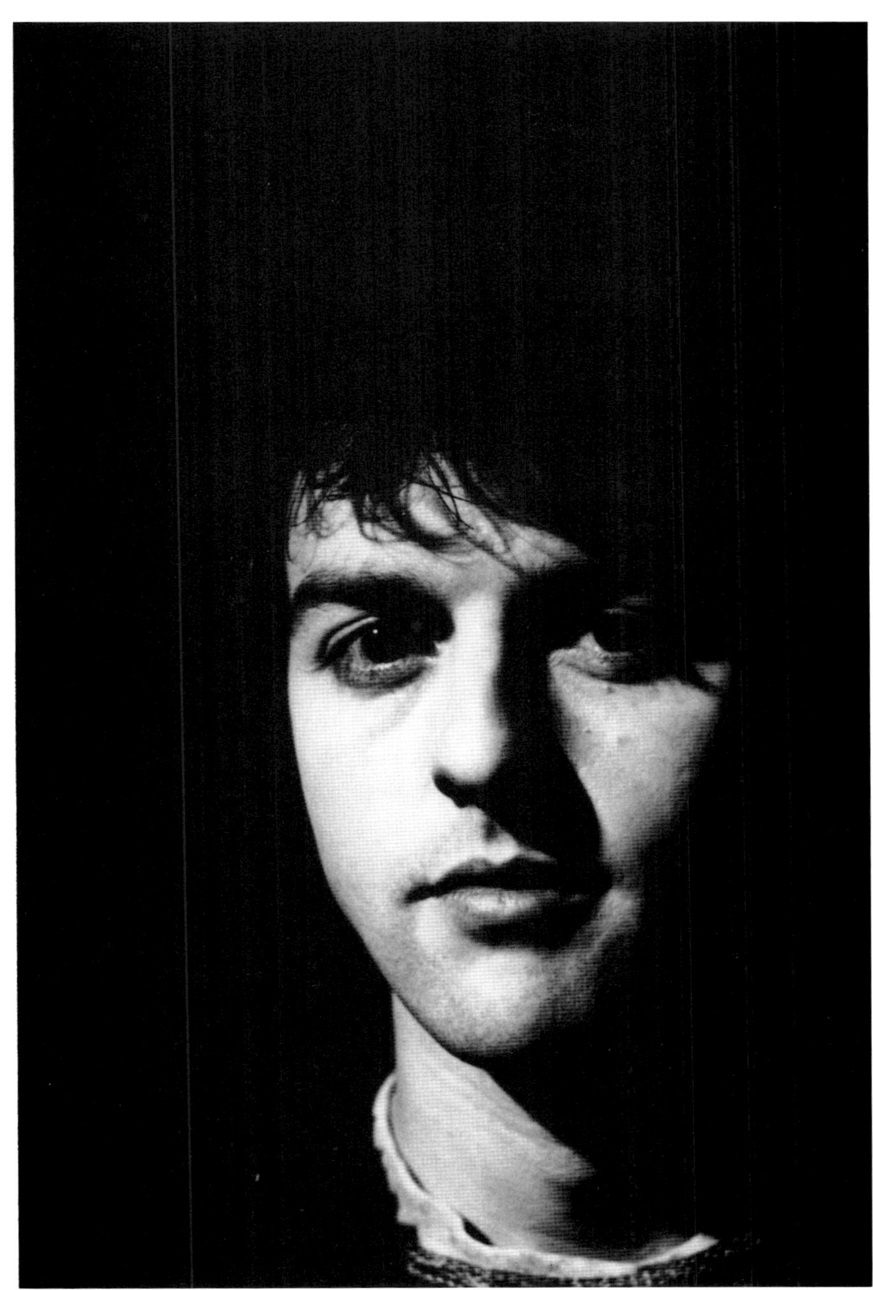

ABBOT
London

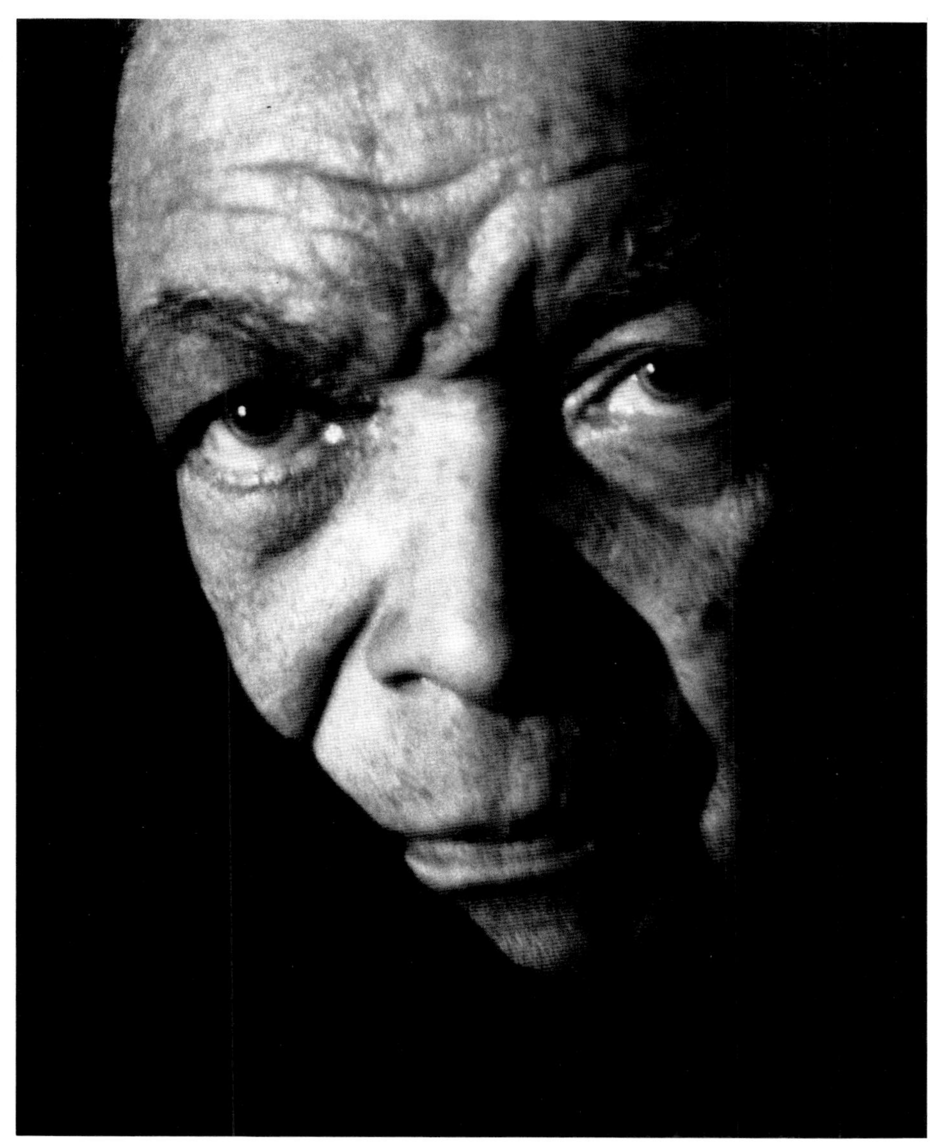

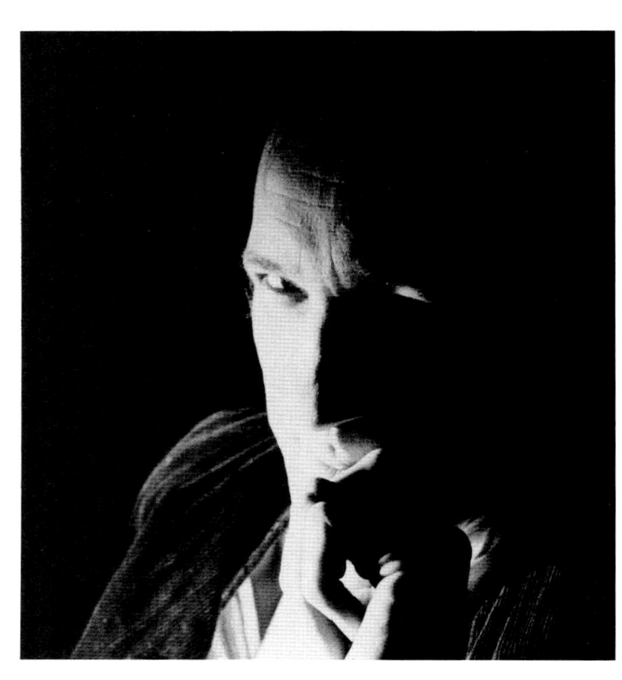

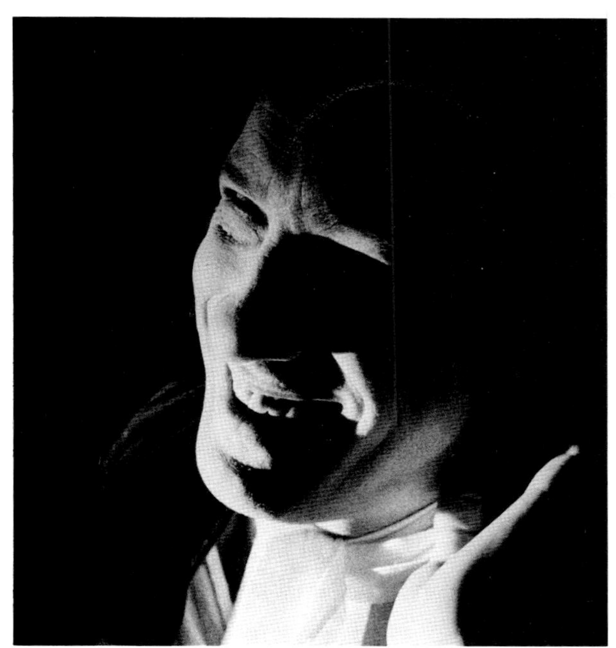

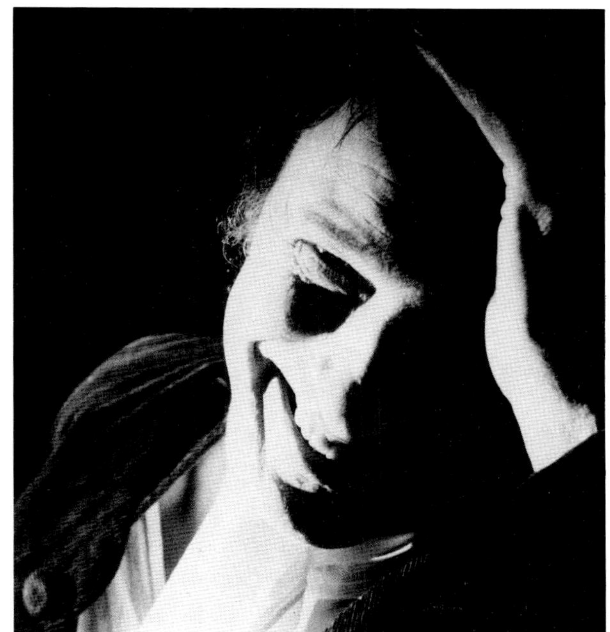

JOHN OTWAY
London

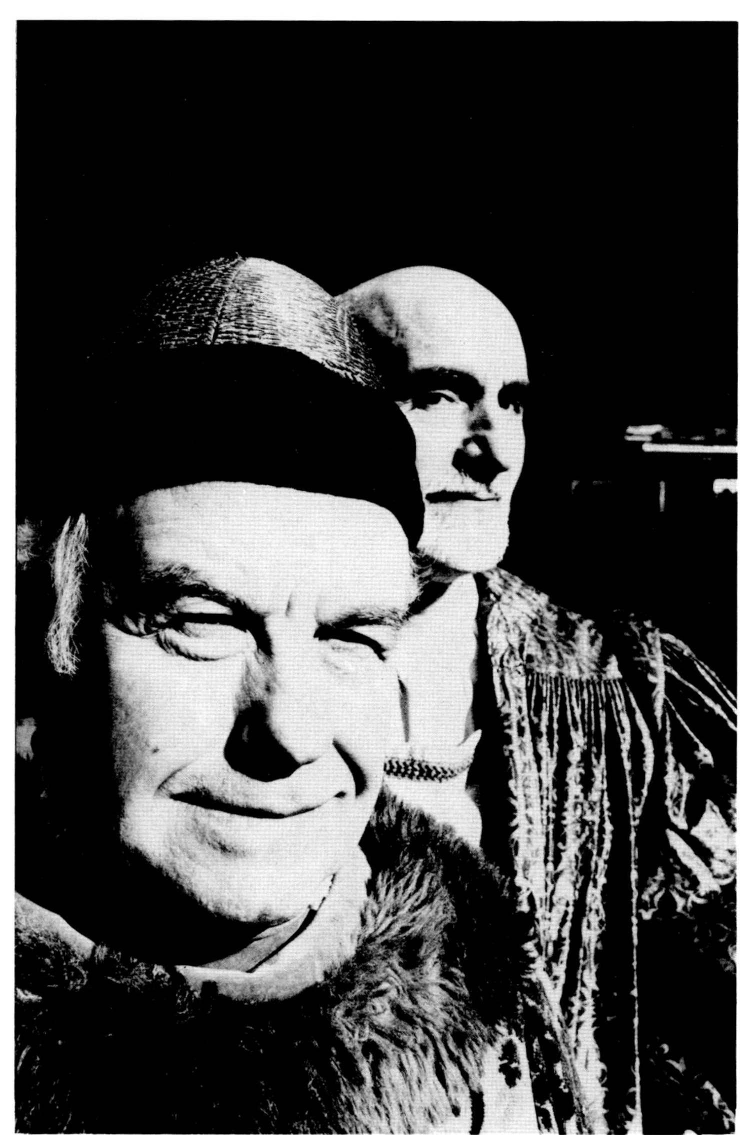

SUSPICION
London

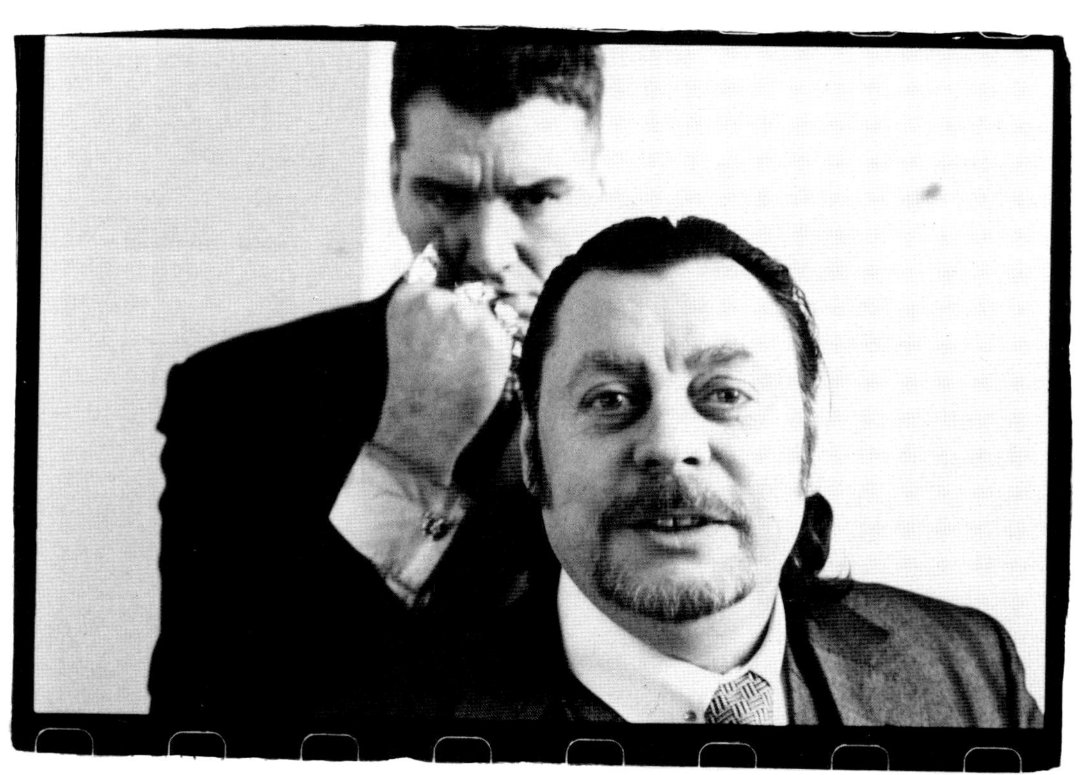

CROUP AND VANDEMAR
London

OLD BAILEY
London

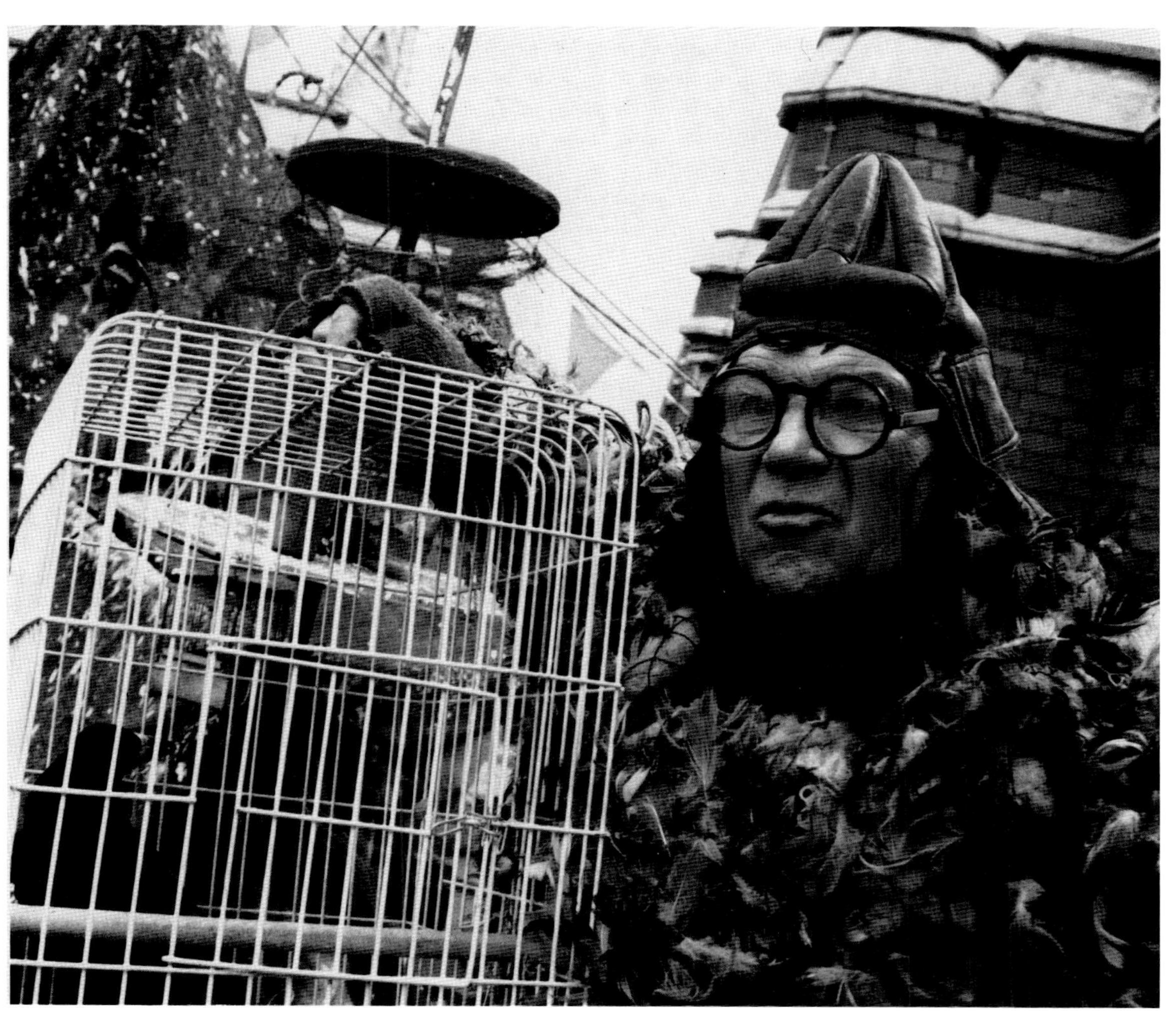

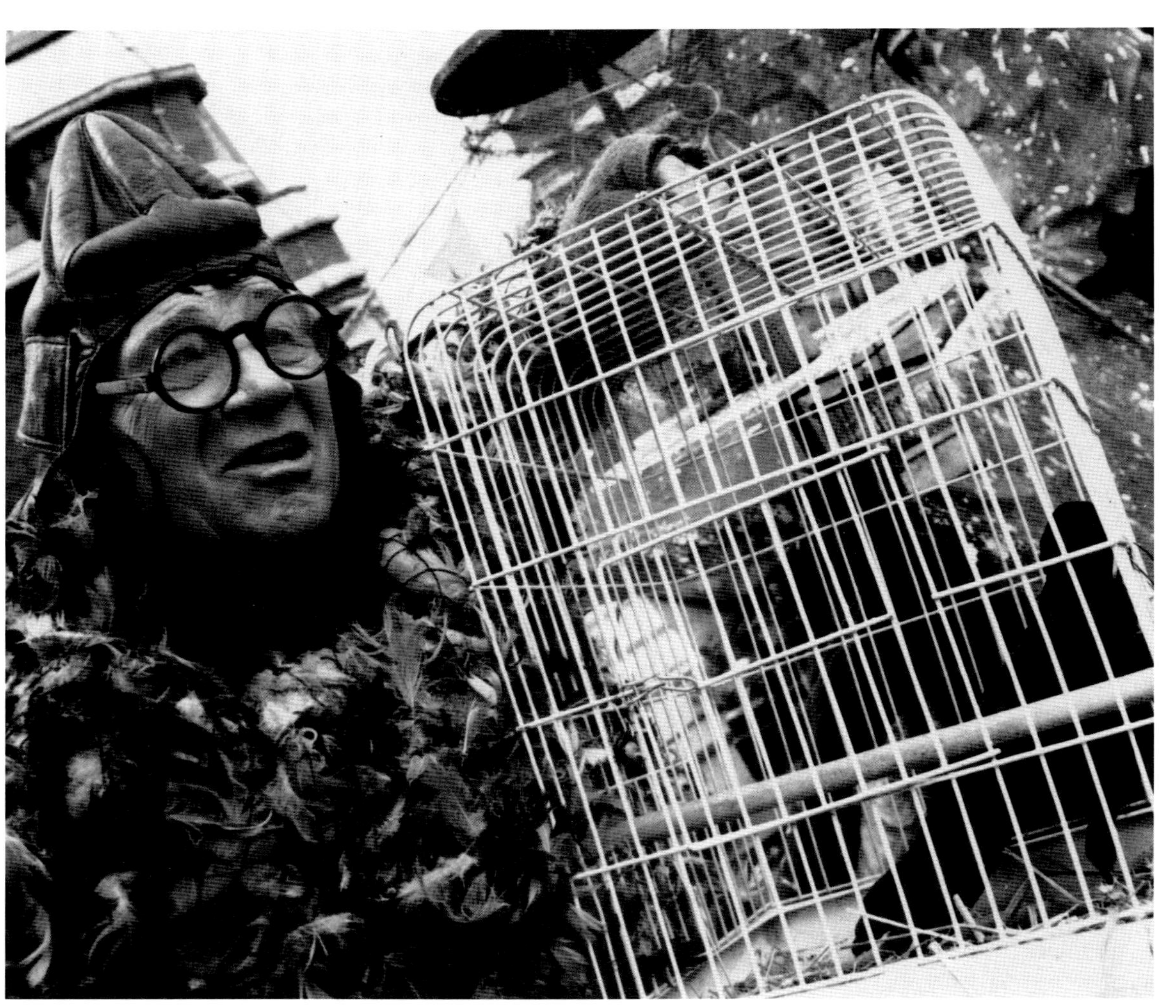

TREVOR PEACOCK
London

ONE AND TWO HALF EXTRAS
London

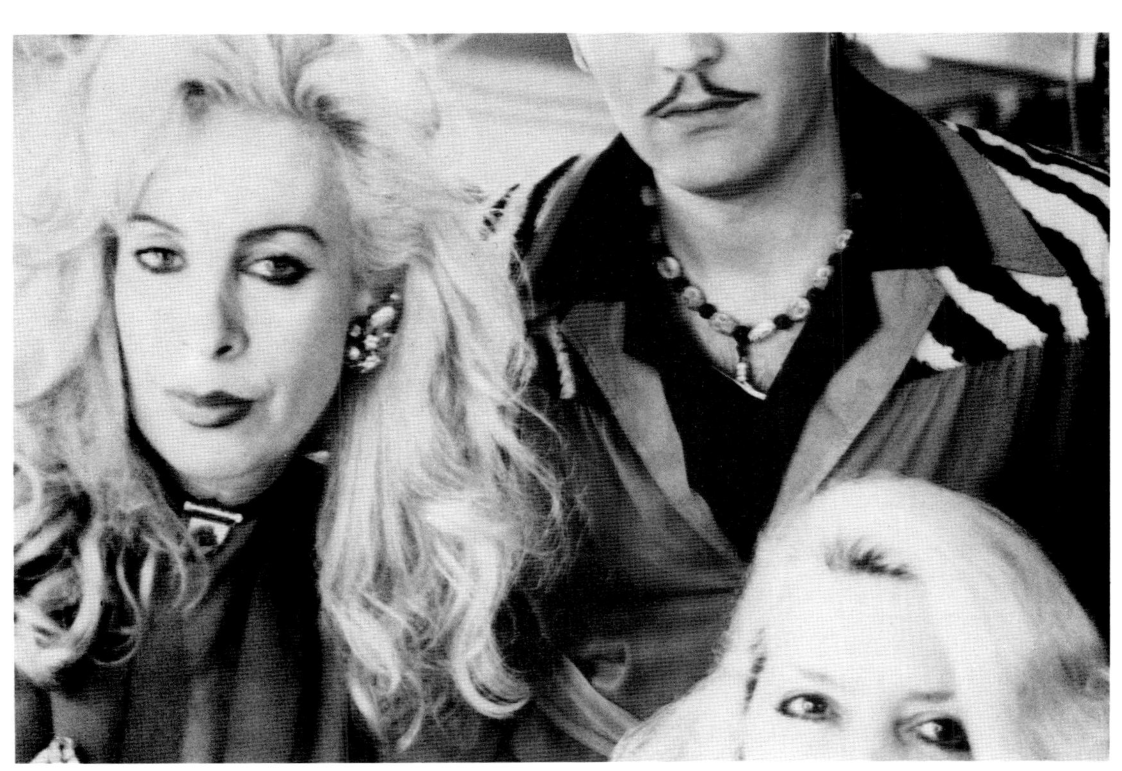

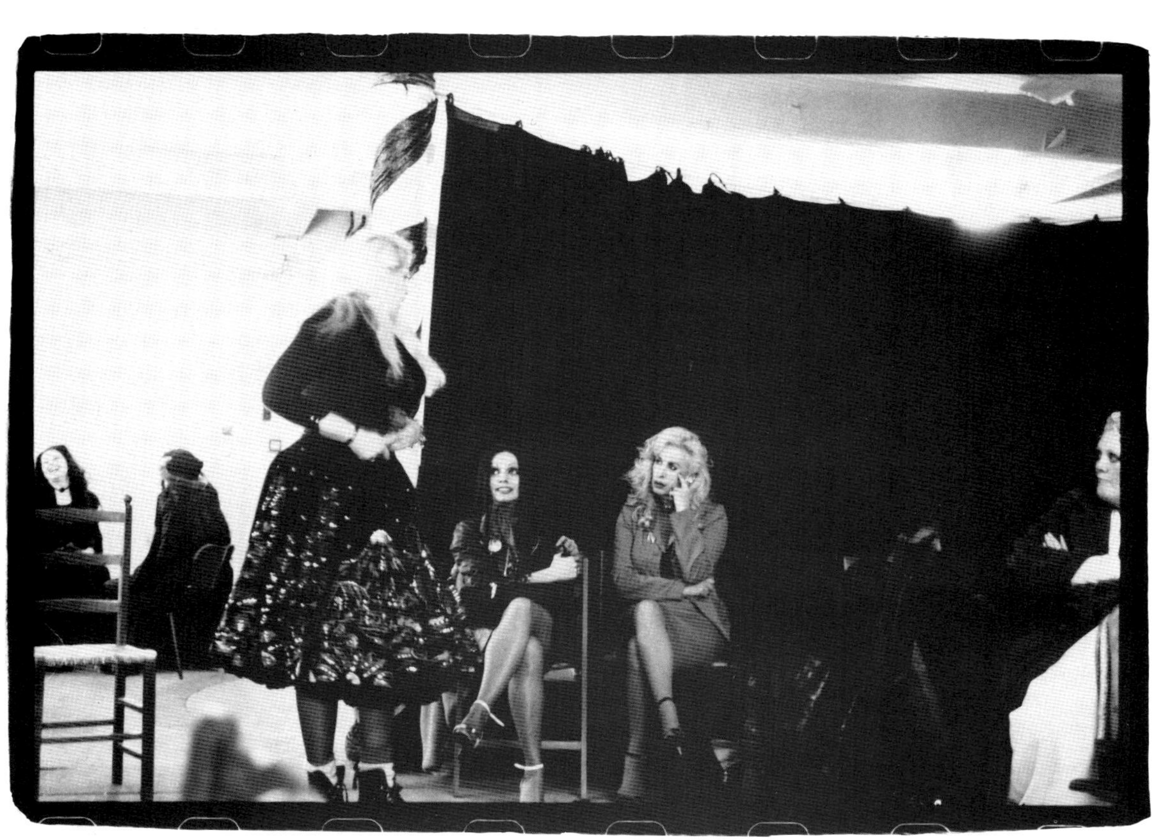

THE DRESS
London

THE CARD GAME
London

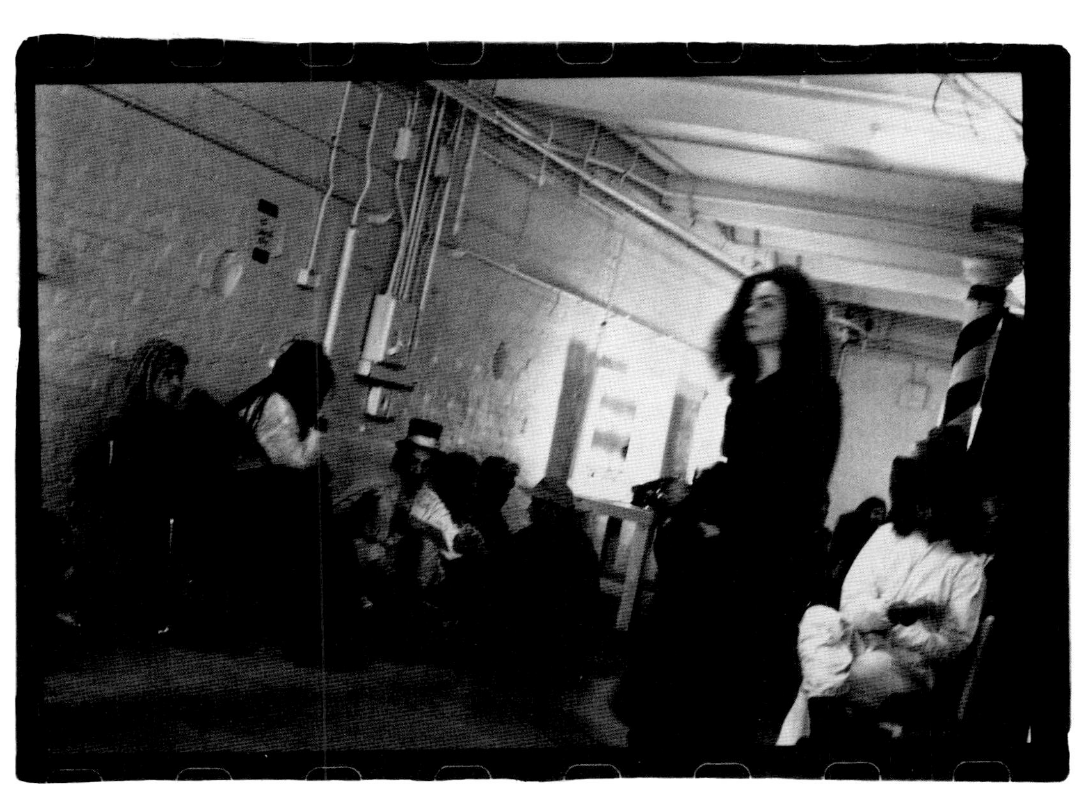

THE CONFESSION
London

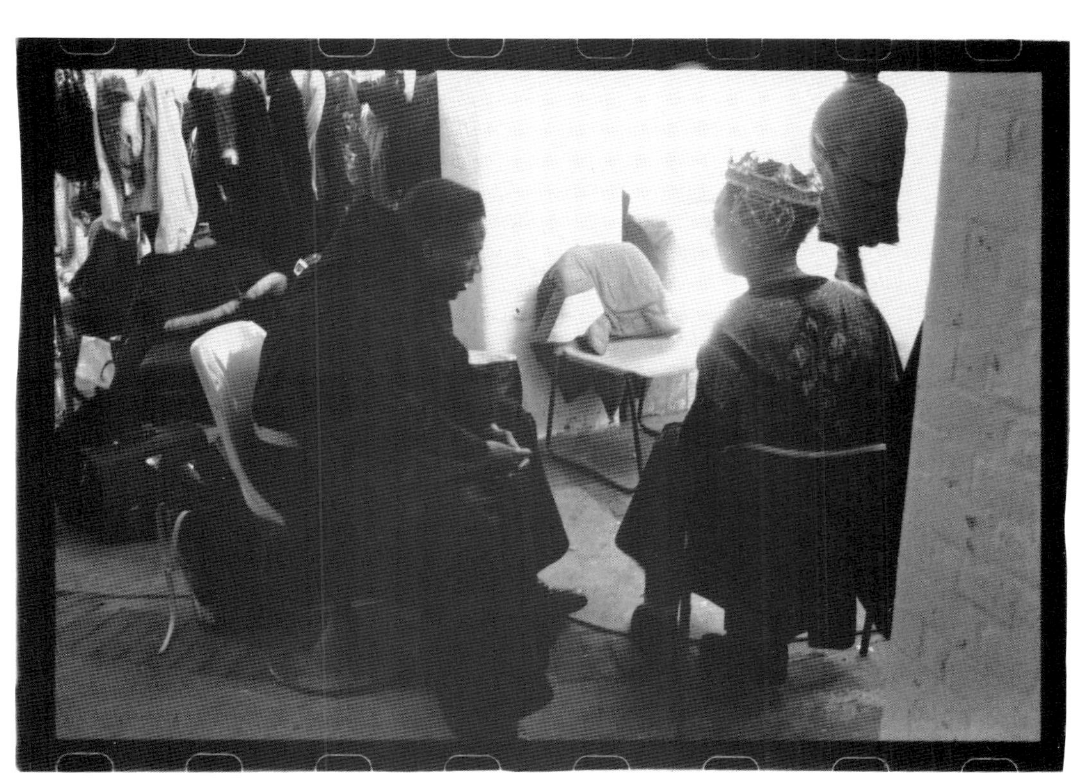

VIDEO
London

ZED'S BODY PIERCING & TATOOS
London

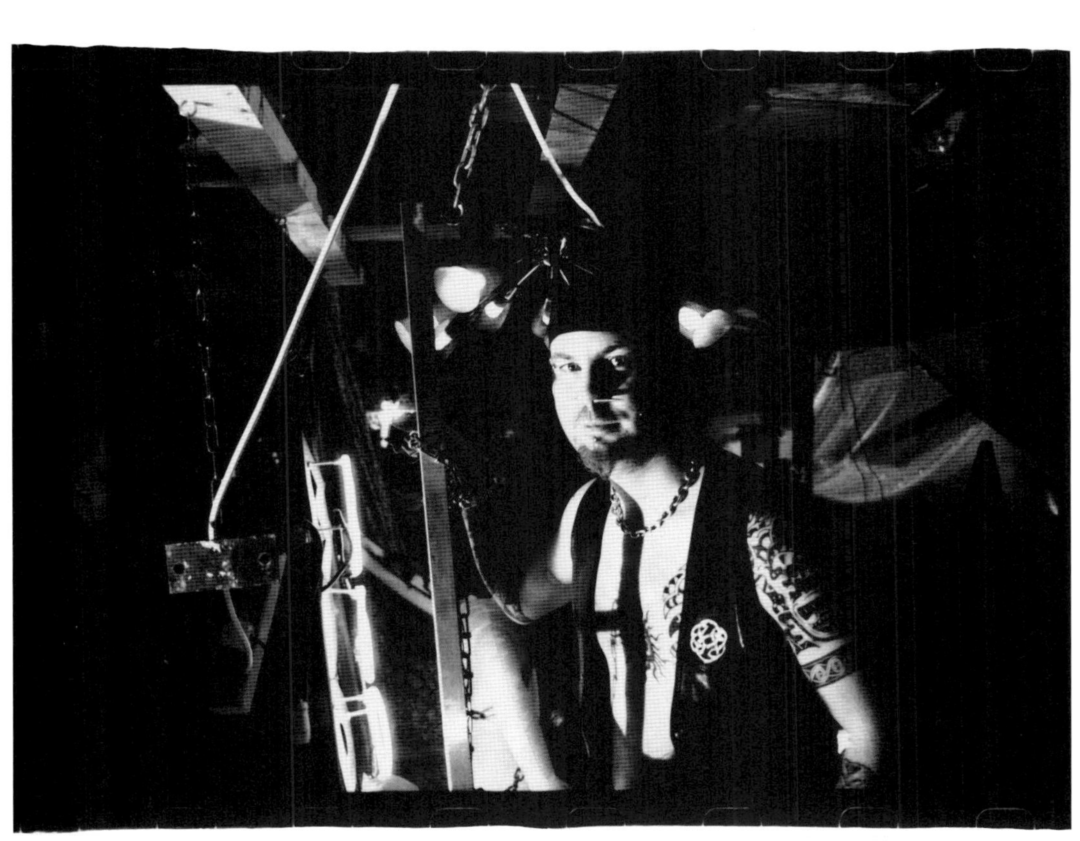

FRENCH TICKLER
London

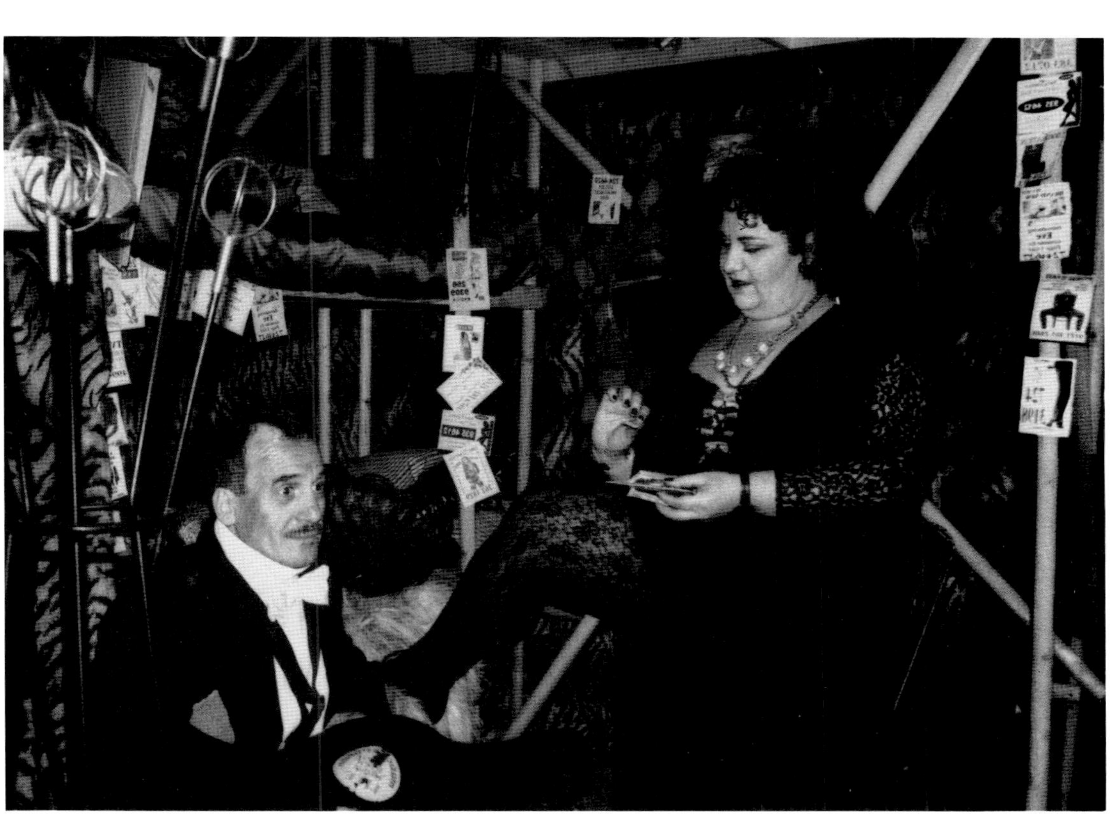

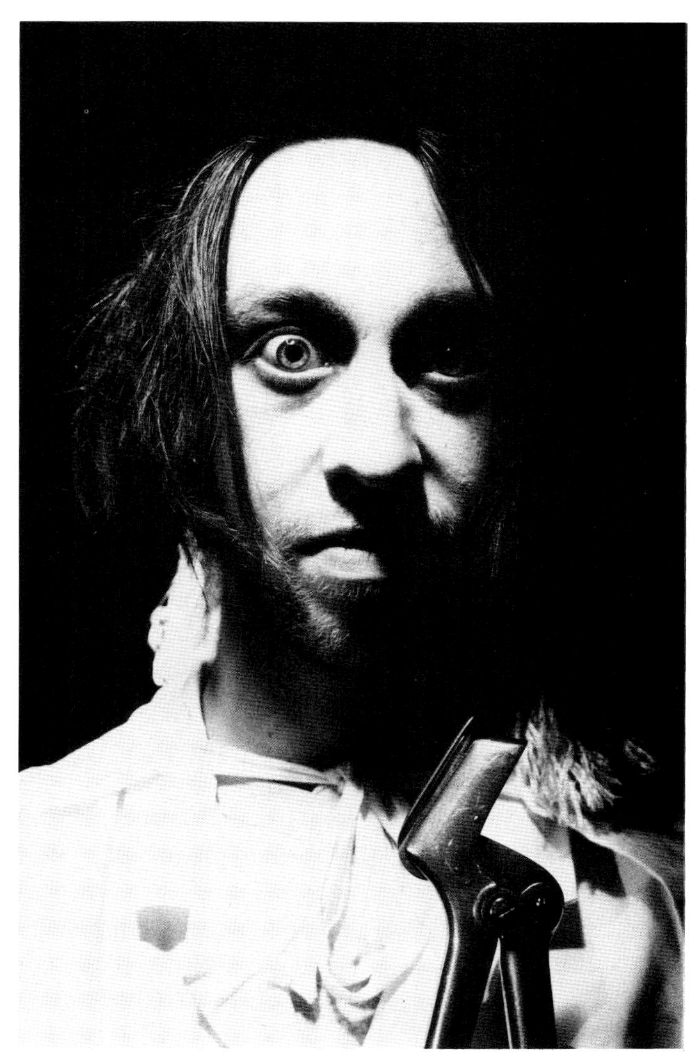

ROOT CANAL
London

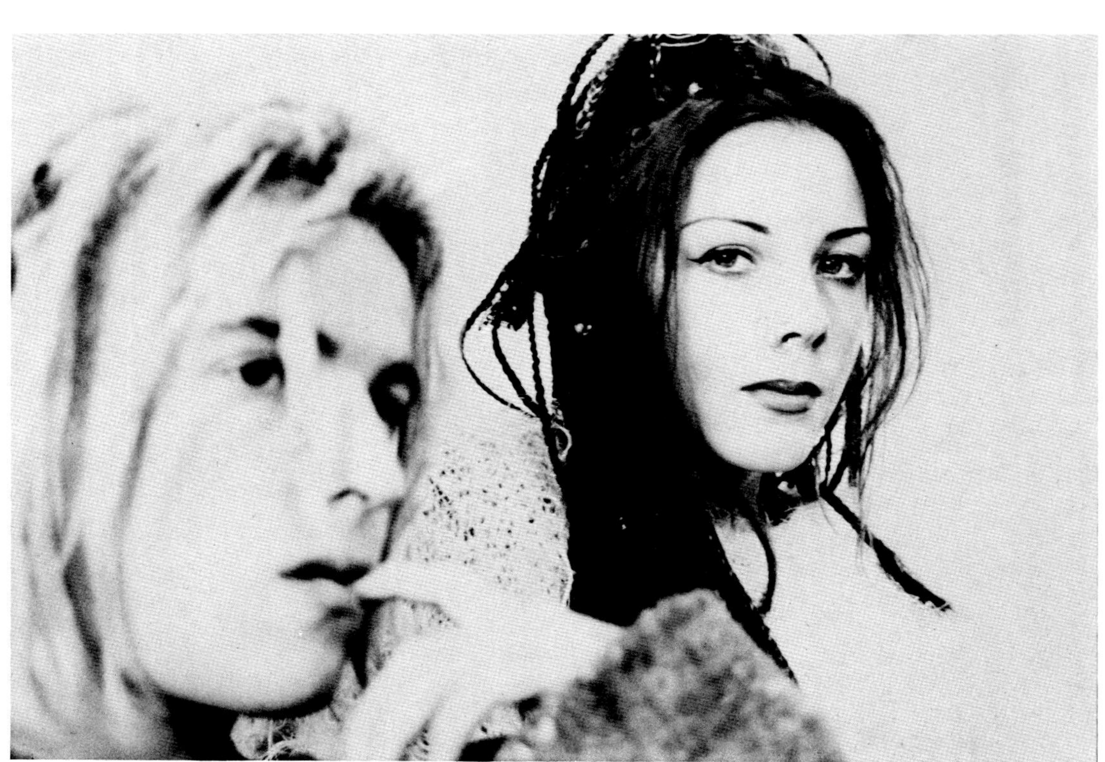

FINGER
London

ROUGES
London

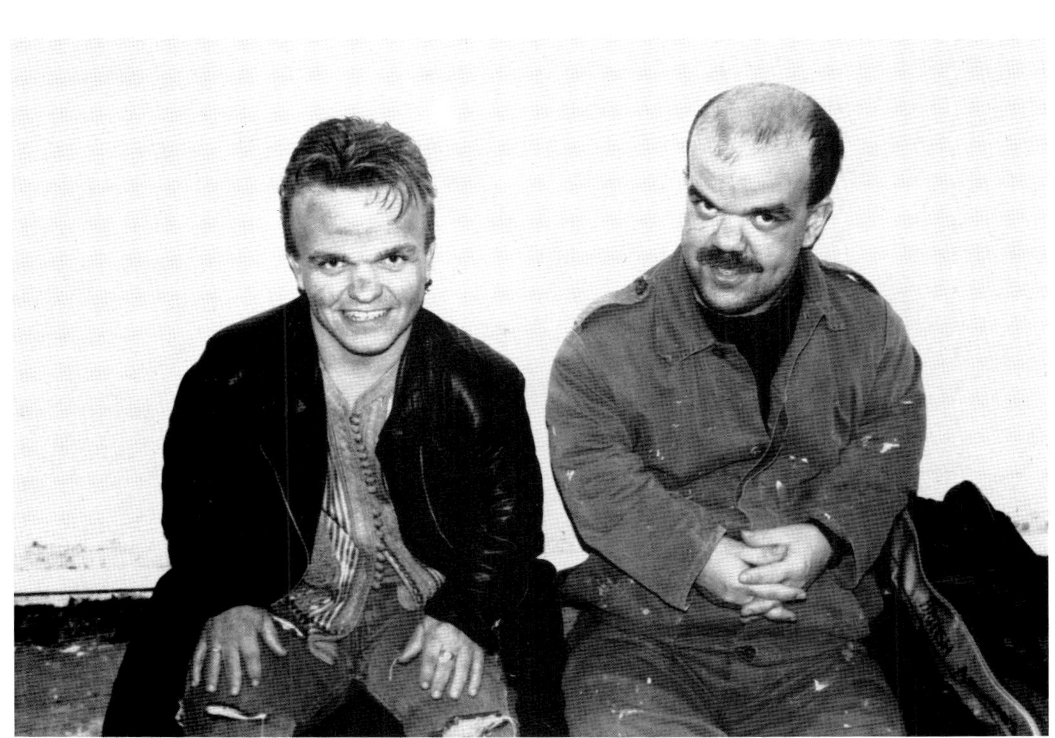

SEWER CHILDREN
London

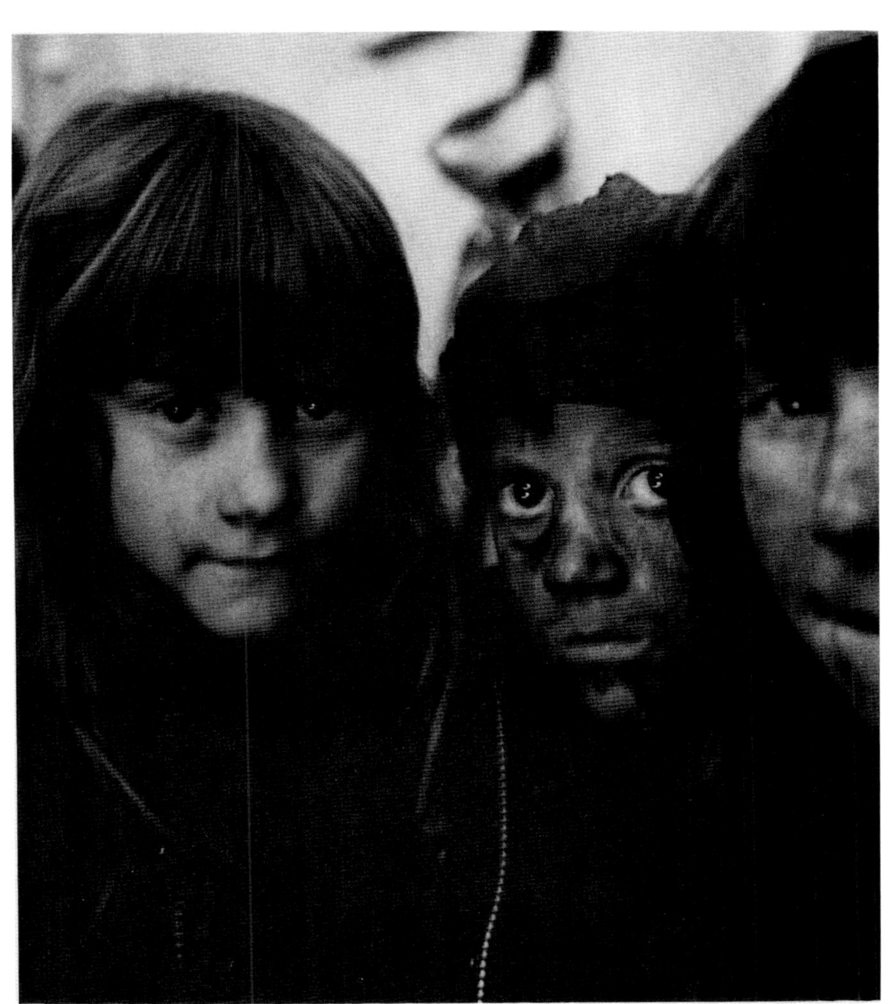

CASSANDRA

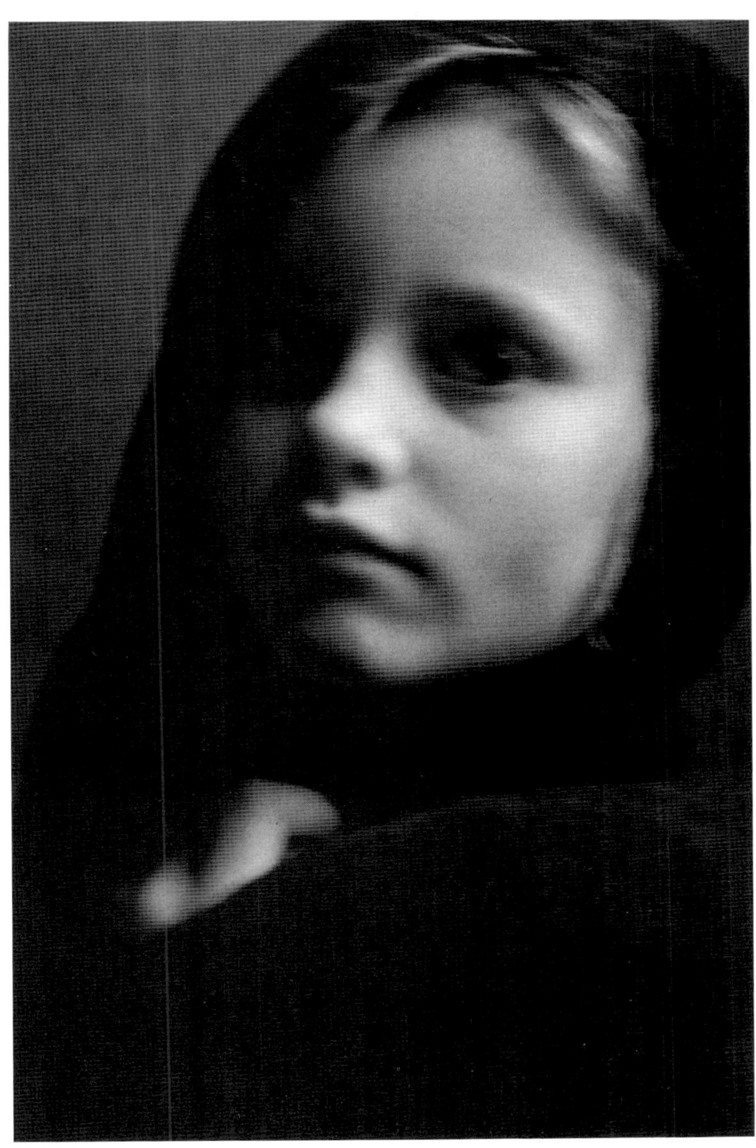

SAFETY PIN
New York

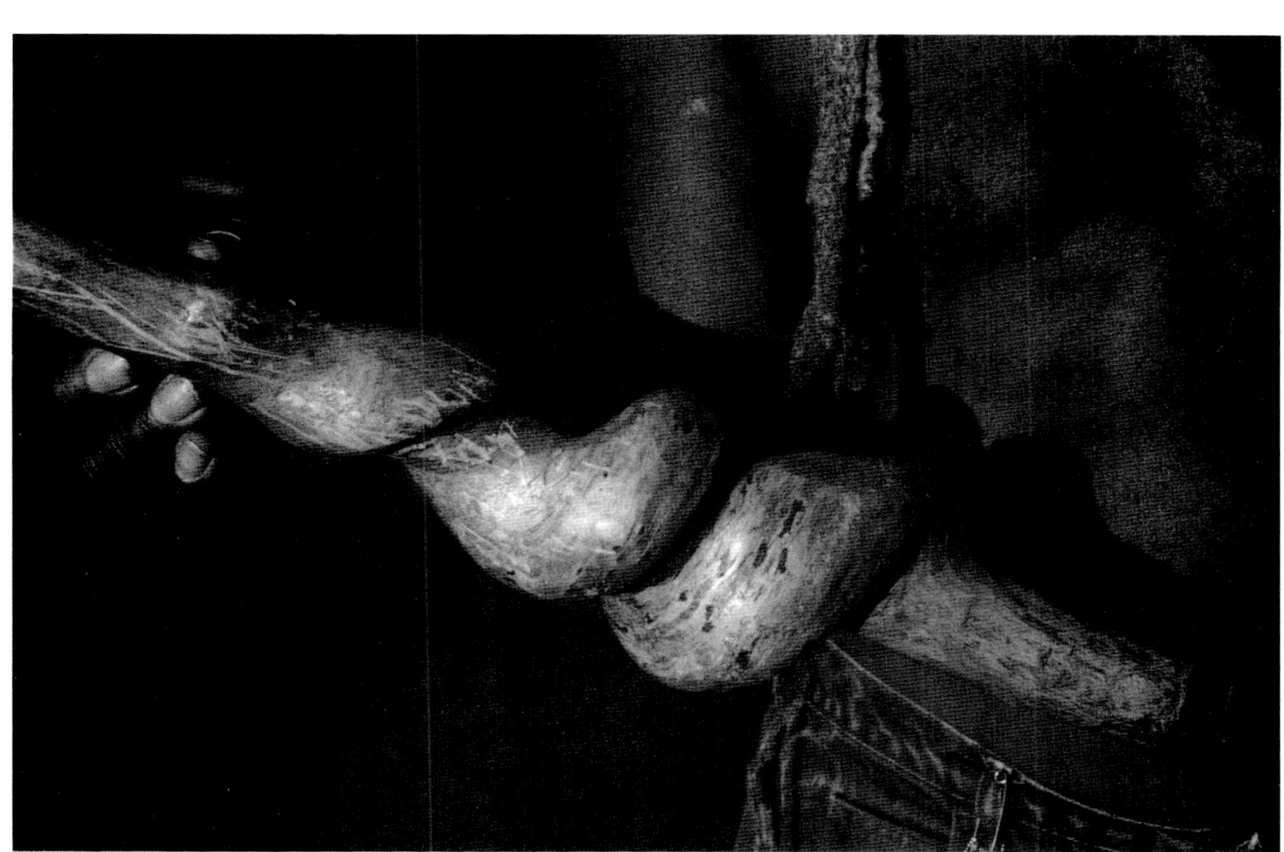

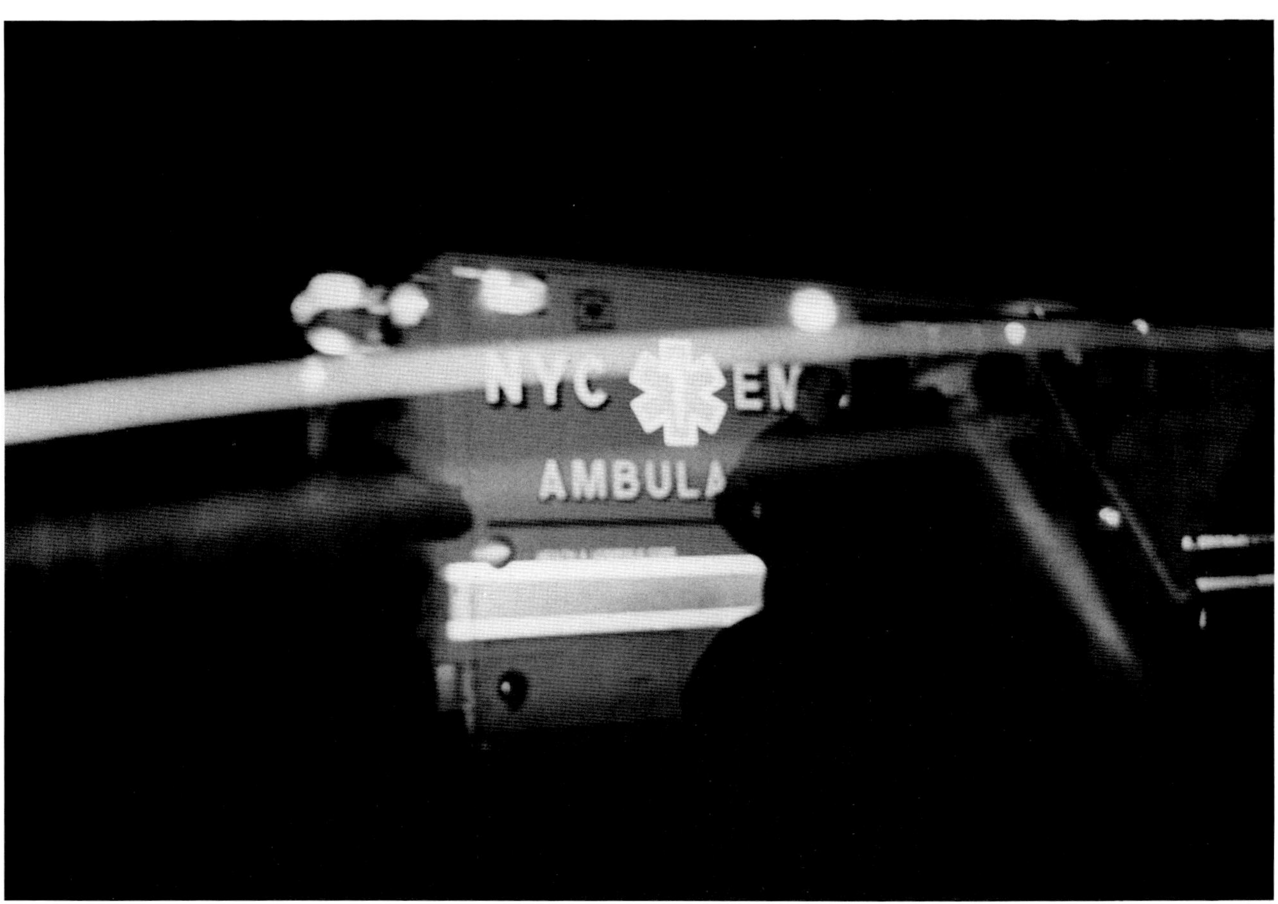
NYC EM
AMBULA

SUICIDE JUMPER ON THE WILLIAMSBURG BRIDGE
May 18 - 1:32 a.m.
New York

A PRINCESS AND A QUEEN
New York
(Overleaf)

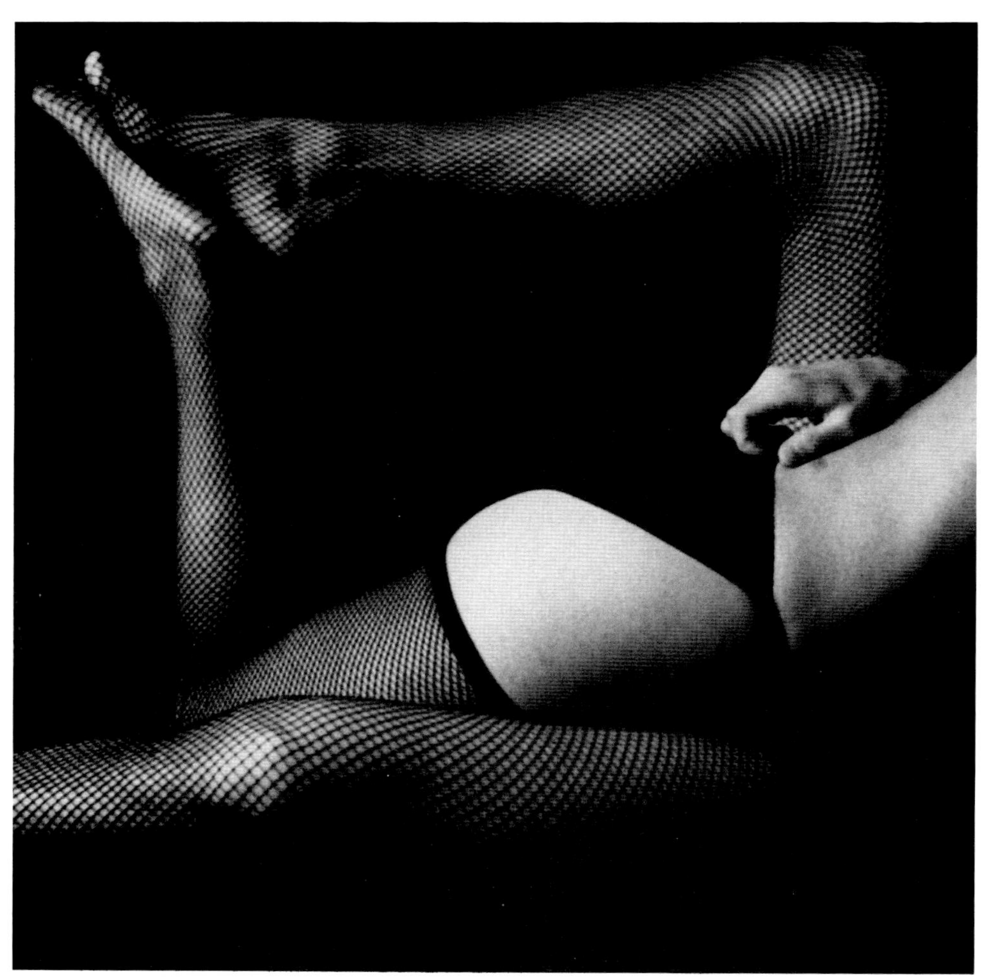

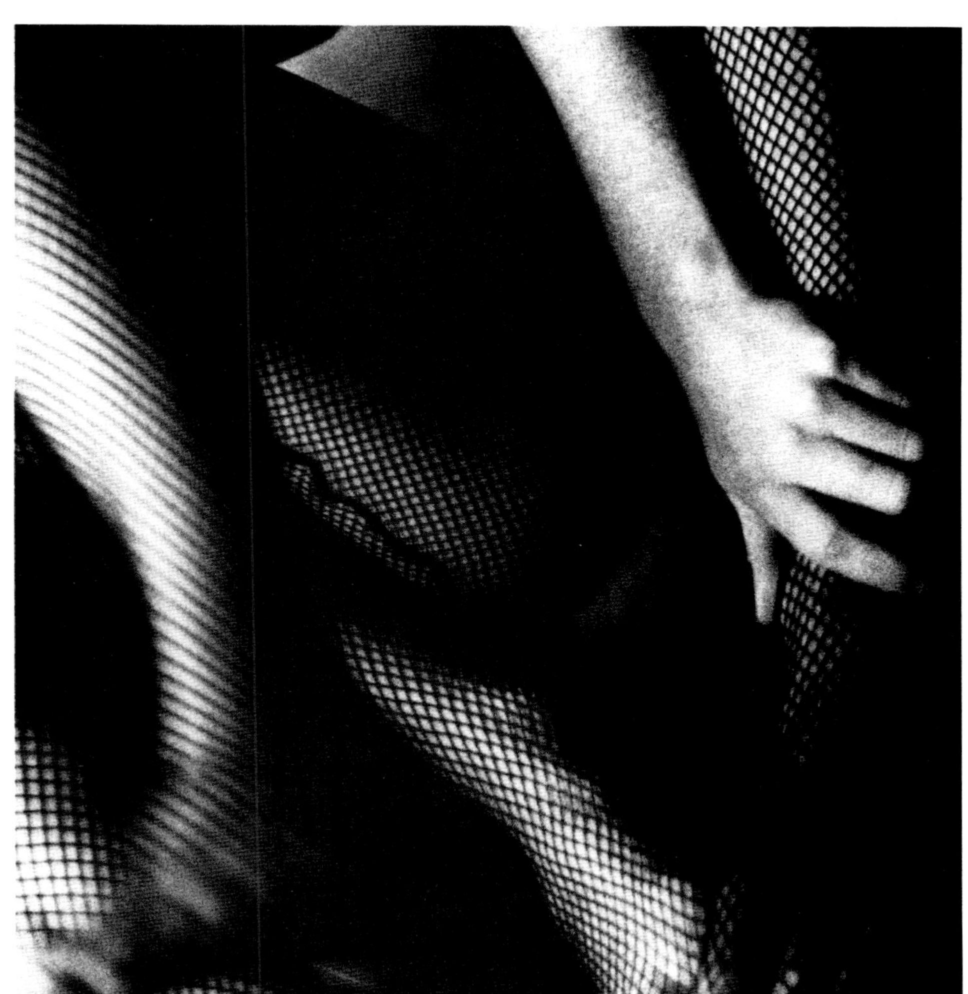

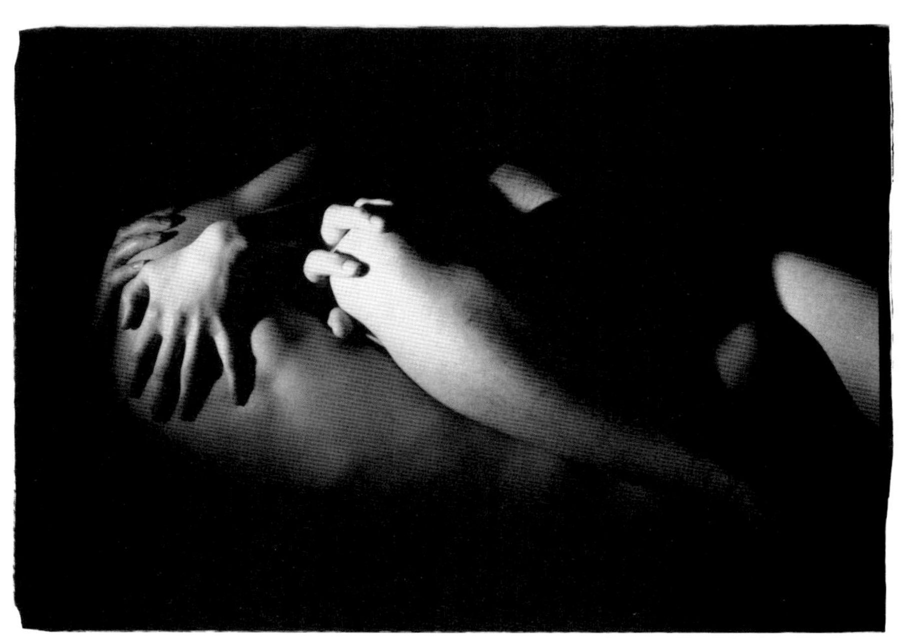

PENETRATION

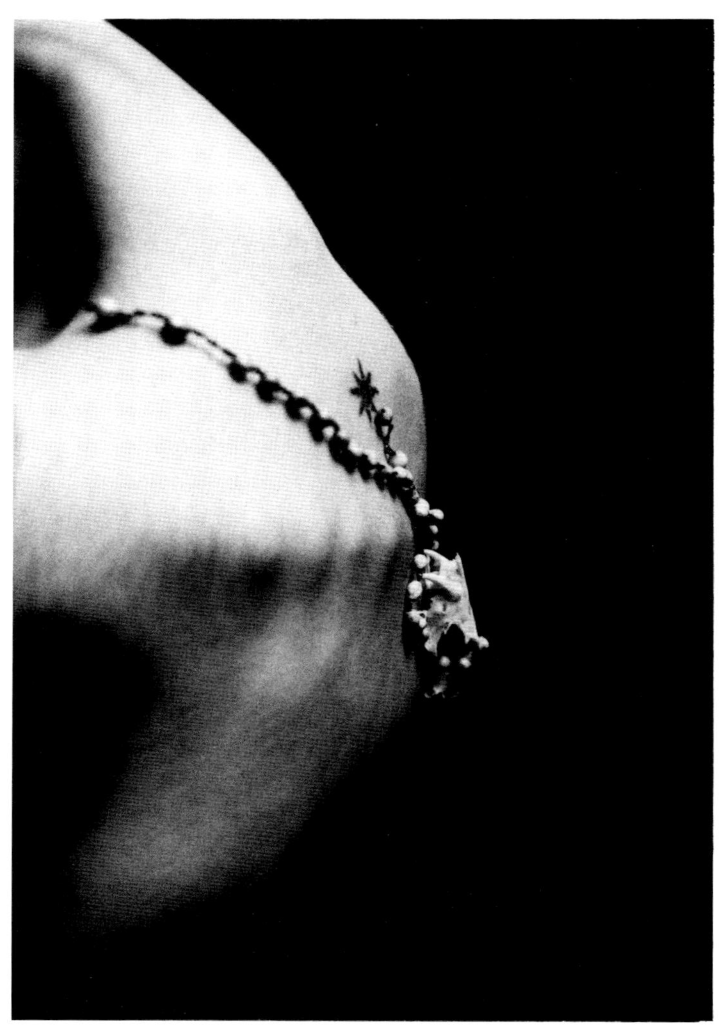

VERTEBRAE
New York

NIPPLE

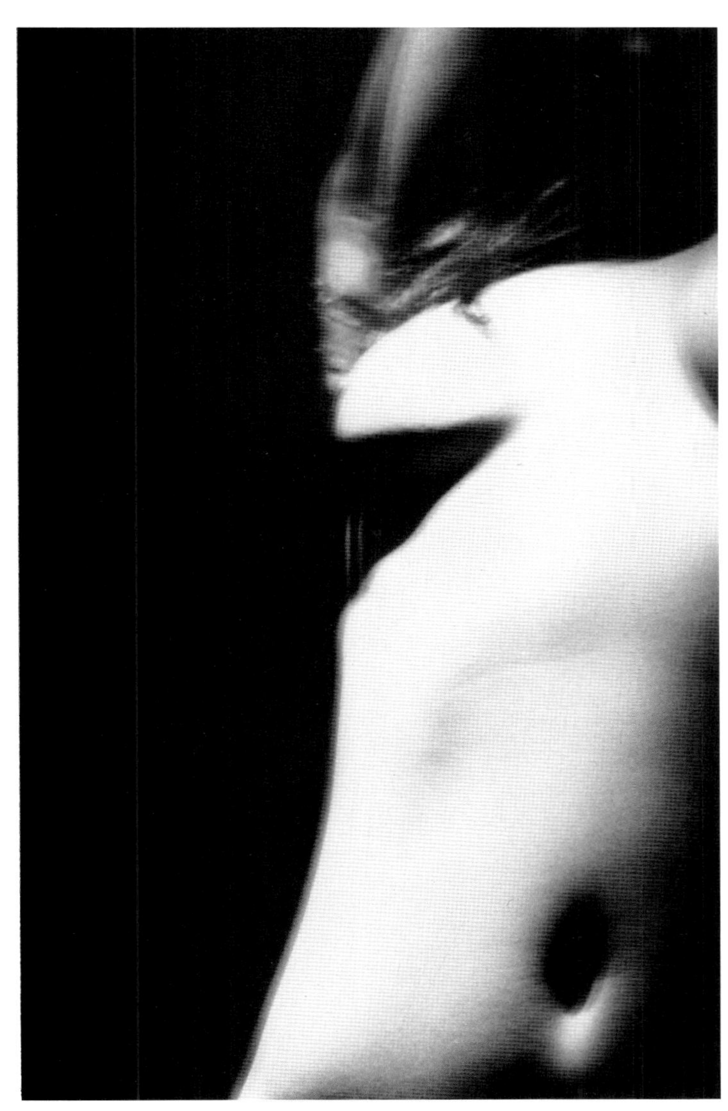

FASHION WHORE

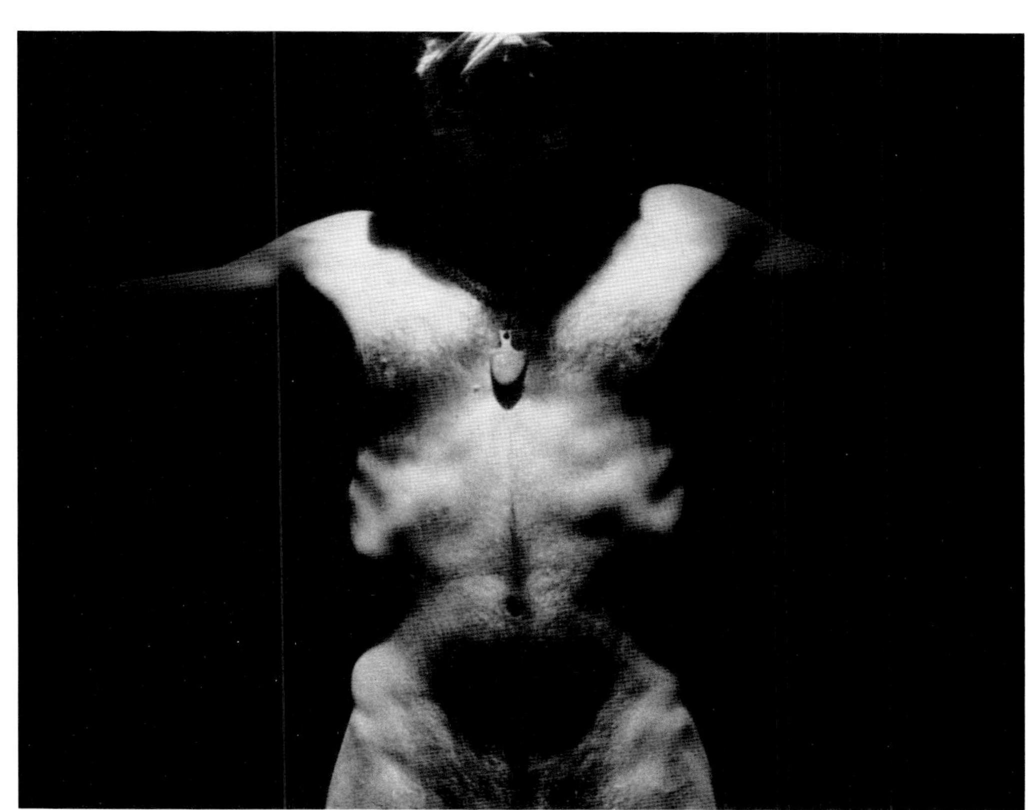

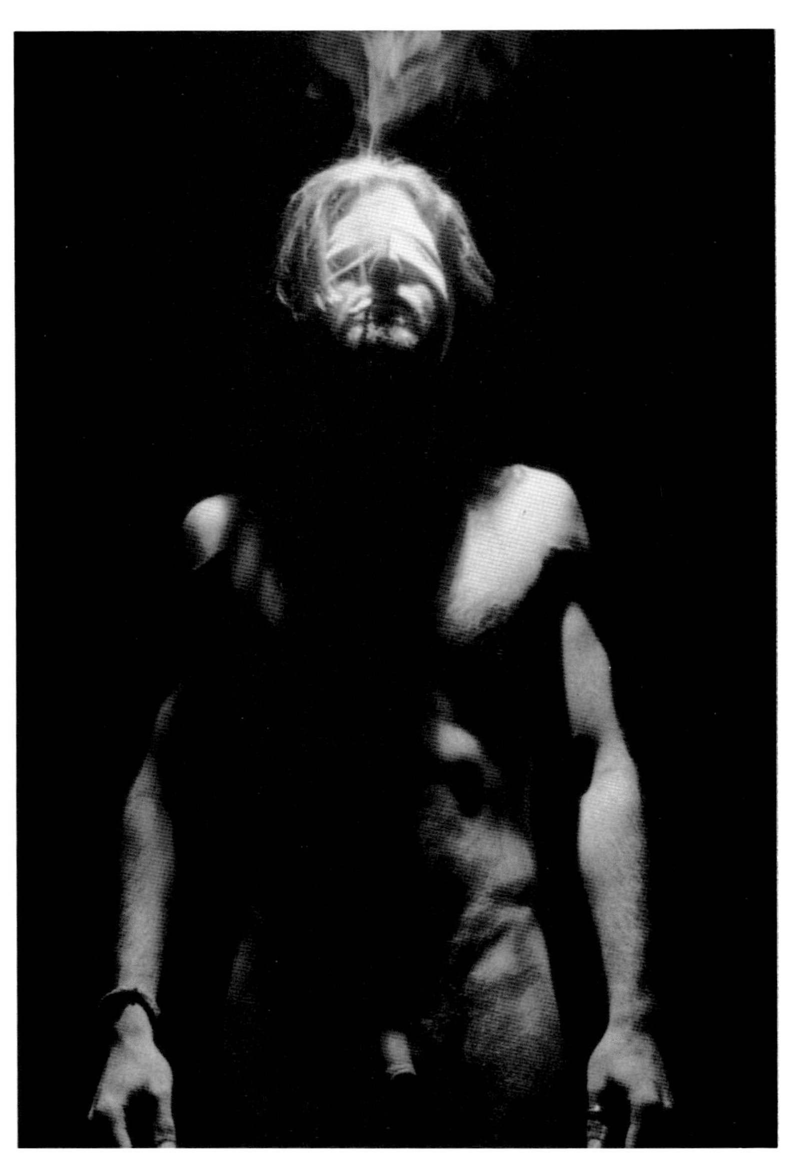

PAUL

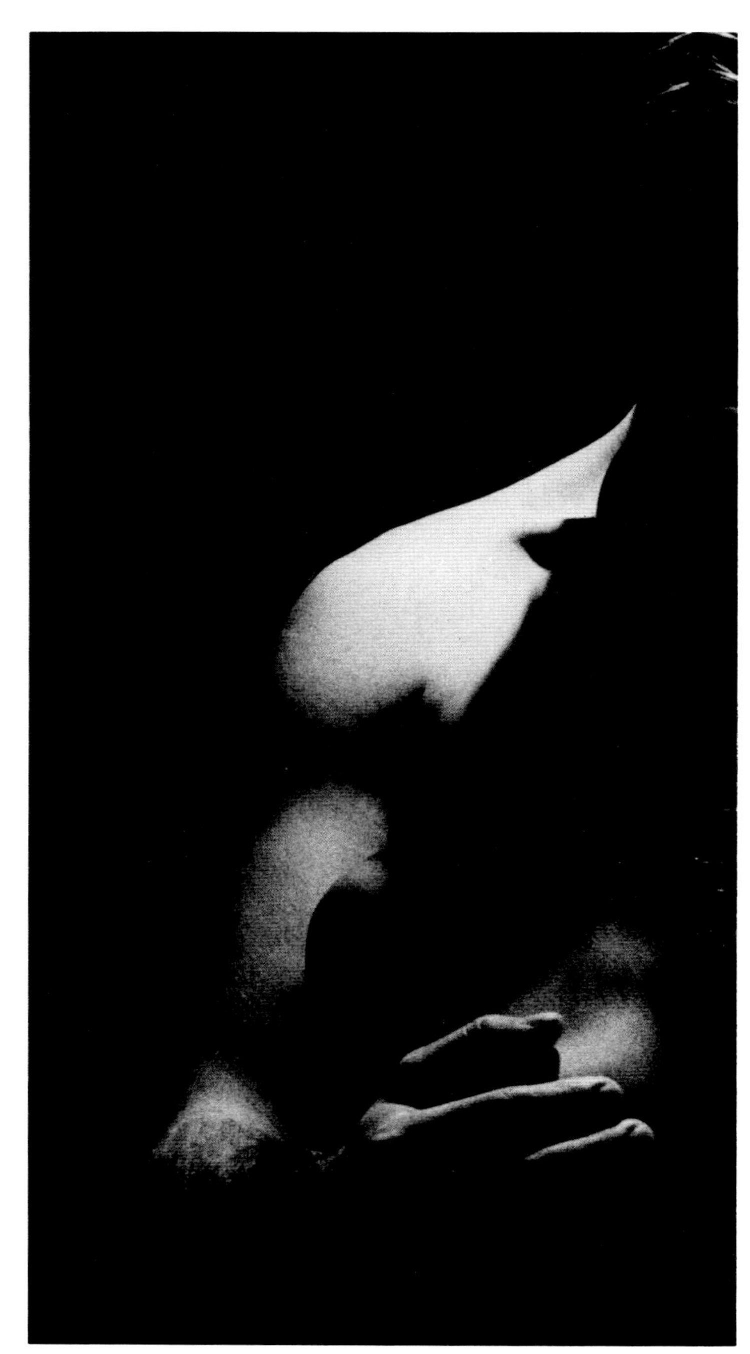

KISS

CANDY CANE
New York

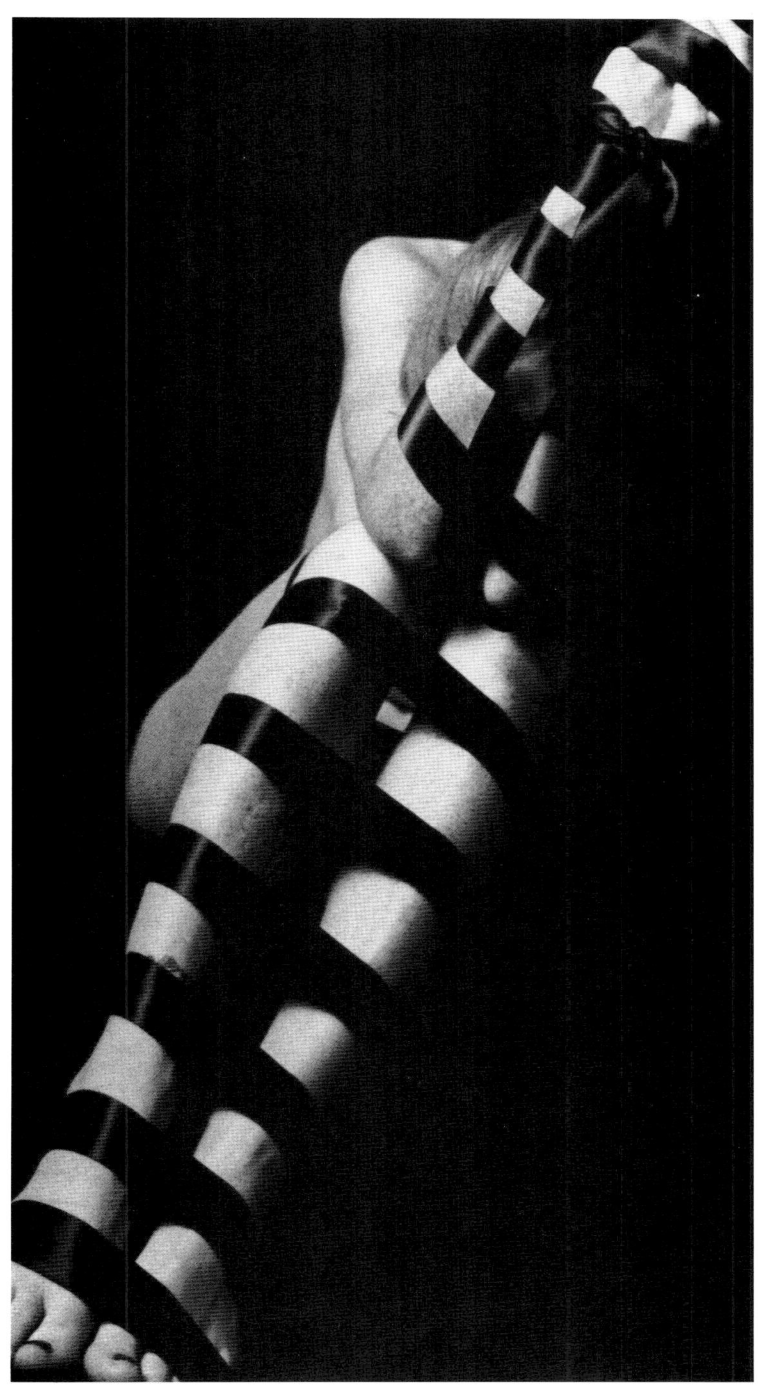

SINGING
London

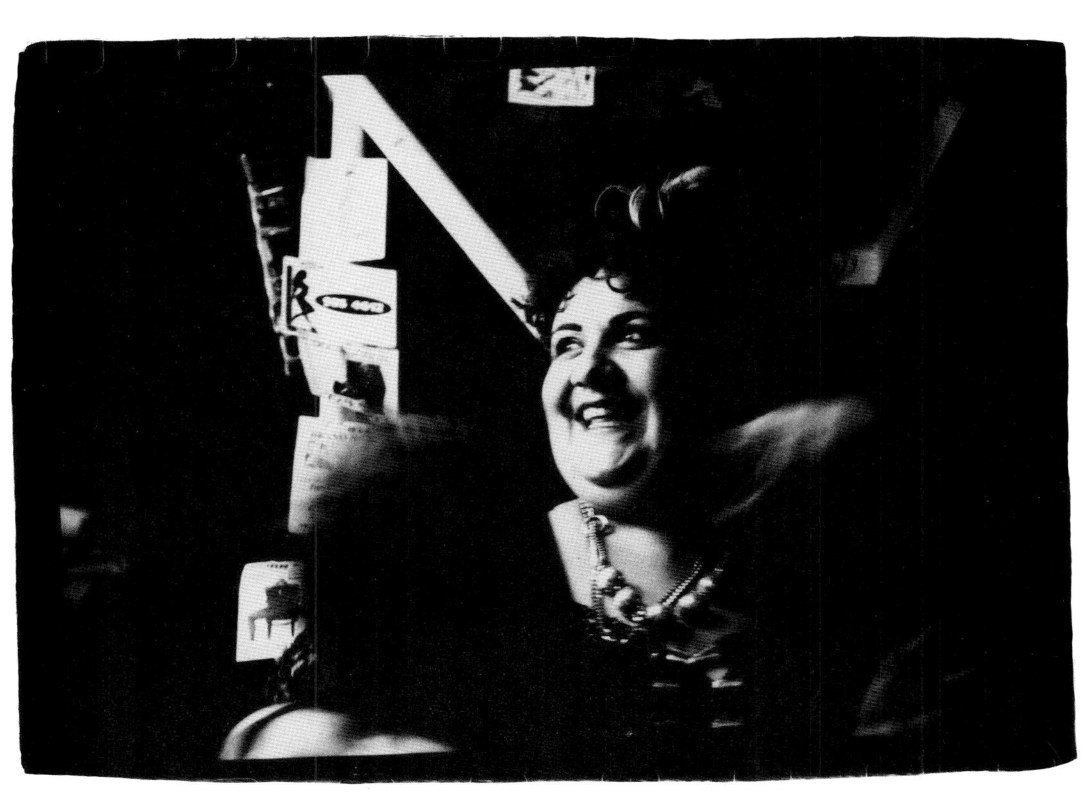

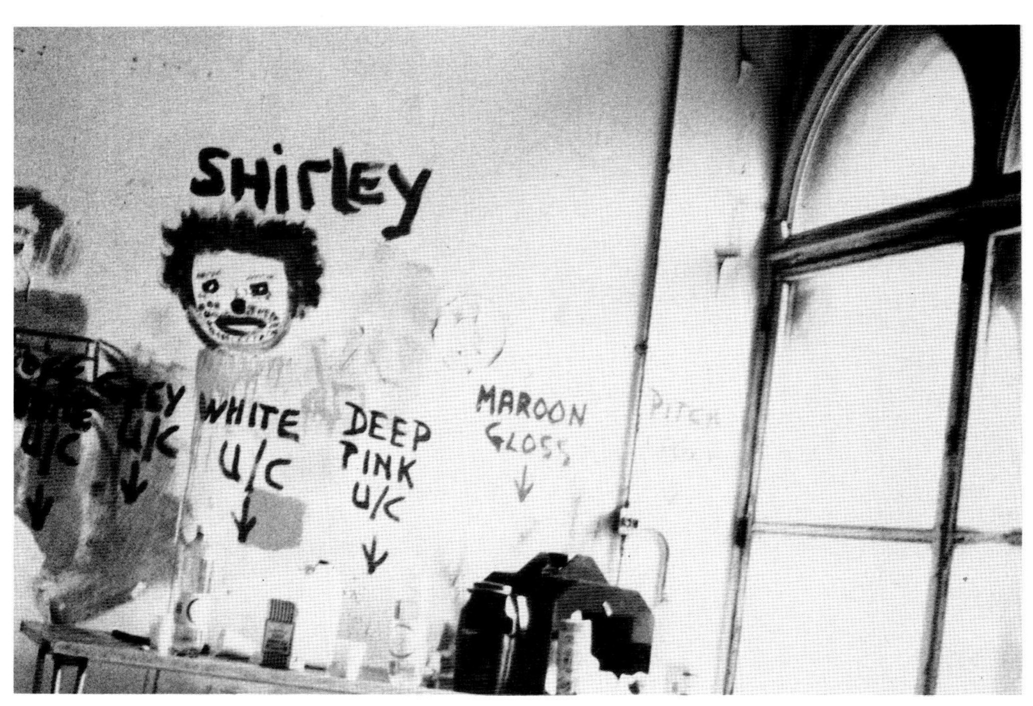
SHIRLEY
WHITE U/C
DEEP PINK U/C
MAROON GLOSS

AFTER WORDS

I am not much of a writer. I tend to see the world in pictures, textures, colors. Perhaps that is why I have surrounded myself with writers, people who can put words to images where I cannot. (I did, however, write a story once. It was called "The Day Elsie's Head Split into Bits". It was about my painted doll, Elsie, and how one day she woke up, looked into the mirror and saw that a crack had begun at her forehead and was making its way slowly down her face. She panicked. She cried. She screamed. She developed a splitting headache and she was terrified. Upon further investigation, Elsie came to the realization that it was the mirror that was broken, not she. Moral: life isn't all it is cracked up to be. End of story.)

That is why I am not a writer. That is why I take photographs and build constructions with found objects or oddities that have been given to me (the best yet was an amazingly Kafkaesque three-inch-bug-thing that made its way to New York from Manila.) Please note: It should be known that my apartment is NOT roach infested. It was merely a curiosity on behalf of the cockroach, which was most likely just visiting, which caused it to peer out from under its hiding place in the sofa as to who this Neil Gaiman character was. It was laid to rest in a haze of fixative fumes, quite happily, I'd imagine.

I have many people to thank: my Mother, for being beautiful; my Father, for a solid foundation; Neil, for being scary; Chris Claremont and Beth Fleisher, for wisdom; the BBC, Crucial Films and the Neverwhere actors and crew, for allowing it to happen; Ben Jorgensen, for whimsy; Jeremiah Wells, for mastering technology; Kris Heintz, Tag, Sara Erickson, for putting up with my endless, nonsensical nonsense; Tom Waits, for brilliance; coffee, for caffeine; Nick Davidson, for loaning me a camera way back when; and to all of the lives and limbs I saw in my lens (especially PB), I couldn't have done this project without any of you.

Kelli Bickman
New York, 1996

To order copies of
What I Thought I Saw
send $23.95 per book plus $3.00 shipping / tax to:

11:11 Studio
PO Box 208-kb
Old Chelsea Station
New York, NY 10113-0208

Original prints available from:

Four Color Images, Inc.
32 Watts Street
New York, NY 10013
phone 1 (212) 431-4234
fax 1 (212) 431-3912

Images in the book were made with a Nikon using a 35-70mm Nikkor Lens.
All photographs were processed and hand printed by the photographer.
No computer enhancement or manipulation was used to change the images in any way.